quick and easy
paint transformations

quick and easy
paint transformations

50 step-by-step ways to makeover your home for next to nothing

annie sloan

CICO BOOKS
LONDON NEW YORK

Published in 2010 by CICO Books
an imprint of Ryland Peters & Small
341 E 116th St., New York, NY 10029
20–21 Jockey's Fields, London WC1R 4BW
www.rylandpeters.com

US 25 24 23 22 21 20 19
UK 25 24 23 22 21 20

A CIP catalog record for this book is
available from the Library of Congress
and the British Library.

ISBN: 978 1 906525 75 0

Printed in China

Editor: Pete Jorgensen
Design: Christine Wood
Photography: Christopher Drake
(Photography on page 51, steps 1 and 2,
and pages 124–125 by Tino Tedaldi)

contents

Introduction

Painting furniture is a tremendously rewarding experience

When I begin a piece of work, I usually have a very vague idea of what I want to do—the color probably, and some broad idea of the technique—but I don't have a really firm idea of the end result. I think it is very important to react to the piece of furniture and not have a plan that you follow rigidly. It is quite acceptable to change your mind because as you paint, the furniture starts to tell you what it wants and needs. The age, texture, and color of the wood, plus the shape and style of the furniture, are all determining factors in how you will paint it. As the first coat goes on, characteristics start appearing and you will begin to have ideas that might differ a little from the original plan. Part of the fun is working with the new inspiration and it is this that will make the piece unique.

Another of my guiding principles is that I also want to paint a piece quickly. Like everybody, I'm busy with lots of activities, so I stop working when I find that I am laboring over something. If I can't think of anything

to do to a piece immediately I will take a break, sleep on it, and come back to it fresh the next day. Sometimes just leafing through some magazines or books, rather than thinking directly about the project, provides me with inspiration.

What starts it off?

I want my piece of furniture to have at least a nodding acquaintance with the past—with old painted furniture from the 18th century or the early 20th century—but I don't want to copy the original techniques exactly. I love 18th-century French, Swedish, and the less fancy Italian painted furniture and I continually make reference to them, but I also adore the crazy, bohemian, expressive artists from the Bloomsbury Group, painting furniture in their Charleston farmhouse during the 1930s. I want to make a unique piece that has character and individuality so I borrow ideas from how old furniture looks now and use my versatile paints to create something new. My take on furniture painting is to look at all the old pieces, remembering that wonderful patina of old age, and then start painting, allowing the furniture to "speak" and let a hint of the random enter the work.

Beauty in imperfection

I do not aim for faultlessness in my work after seeing the most charming piece of painted furniture I had ever set eyes on in the Doge's Palace in Venice—a captivating découpage cabinet built in the 18th century. None of its lines were straight or measured and the paper cut outs were not completely stuck down. It was dark in some places, faded in others, and worn in parts, but the sum of these inconsistencies was a certain sort of perfection. This was a lesson for me. Of course I don't want furniture to look rough and uncared for either and there is a fine line between distressing and destroying. Part of the ability to achieve this look is learning to work with color.

Color choices

Color combinations are probably the most important thing to get right. Hard contrasts, lots of colors without an anchor, too many hot colors, or too many same-toned colors are all things I try to avoid when working. If you are not confident with color a good rule is to try using just two colors, or three at the most. It is best if they are different tones, with a middle note or tone for most of the piece and a light and a dark tone for

a high note and a base. The fashion at the moment is for pale colors with some joyous color in parts. Maybe your furniture could be the colorful highlight in the room. Or paint the wall in a strong color and have the furniture light and subtle.

Choosing the furniture

Use decent furniture to begin with. Don't try painting a tea trolley and expect it to look like it came from a French château. The furniture just has to be the right shape, so reproduction pieces are perfect. Don't be put off by furniture that has a bad finish or small pieces missing, but don't get carried away as replacing too much can be time consuming, dull, and frankly not worth it unless the piece is really exceptional. Wood glue will stick down lifted veneer and loose molding, and plaster can fill gaps. Remember that paint will hide water-damage stains and horrible colored wood. Using my paint (see page 154) means I do not usually have to rub down the piece of furniture or prime it, so I can just get stuck right in and start doing the interesting bit.

Enjoy, enjoy, enjoy!

tools and
materials

PAINT Make sure you get the right paint for the job. This will open up a lot of possibilities and make painting your furniture a pleasant experience, because the paint will be responsive and you will be able to work in a practical flexible way. There are many house paints on the market but I believe that my purpose-made paints (see pages 154–155) are the best for the projects in this book. They have been specially created to be used in a whole variety of ways—for example, as a wash, with or without texture, or applied thickly. The paint has a very matt texture and absorbs wax easily, plus you don't have to prime the furniture or rub it down in preparation, meaning you can start painting easily and quickly while you have the urge. The paint, despite being water based, even mixes easily with the solvent-based wax too, so you can color the final finish to get the exact color you want to achieve. For the most part with my Chalk Paint® you only need to apply one coat, but where two coats are necessary apply the first one with a big brush.

COLOR Working with a good palette of colors is important, as is being able to mix them. I use a palette of ready-mixed neutrals with stronger colors, working on the premise that you can lighten strong colors but can't make a light color strong. My already-aged colors, such as Duck Egg Blue, can be lightened with Old White, but for colors like Provence, which is rather clean, it might be better to add Country Grey to dull it and give it a little complexity. Of course, waxes can change the color too, so take this into consideration when you are applying your chosen paint.

Color is extraordinary because it changes so much according to the context within which it is used—a color that looks great in one room could look like dirty pondwater in another because of light (either artificial or natural) and the surroundings. Don't worry if your initial choices do not give the effect that you hoped for—with the methods in this book you can change the tone and color of a piece using washes and colored waxes.

BRUSHES Your brush does not have to be expensive, but it does need to have certain qualities because working with bad brushes can be very detrimental. I find that using a brush that is a mix of synthetic and bristle is the best. The hairs should be fairly long and flexible with a little bounce to allow you to be expressive in your work.

I don't usually like to have a list of "do nots" but this one seems useful and may help to highlight any possible problems:

• Don't work with brushes that are too short since the paint will not flow well.

• Don't use a brush with hard and inflexible bristles, because the paint will look scratchy.

• Don't have a floppy brush, because you will have to work too hard to make the paint spread.

• Don't use a really cheap brush because the hairs keep coming out and that is just plain annoying!

• Don't work with just one rather small brush since this quickly becomes tedious. Have a collection of brushes to hand, such as a large one at least 3–4in (7.5–10cm) wide for painting onto the furniture with speed and a smaller 1–2in (2.5–5cm) brush to get into the intricate parts, including moldings and corners. In the projects in this book, I tend to work with a 2in (5cm) and 1in (2.5cm) brush, but pick a size that feels comfortable for you to use.

WAXES, SANDPAPER, VARNISHES, AND CLOTHS I wax more or less everything I paint to get the right finish for my furniture and walls. I find it makes my projects strong and practical and gives them a beautiful workable finish. I recommend that you choose a soft wax that can be applied easily with a brush. I generally use a 1in (2.5cm) brush in the projects to apply wax, but you can use a large brush to get it done quickly if it feels more comfortable. After adding a layer of clear wax to a piece, you can then start applying dark wax or coloring the clear wax with some of my paint to alter the finish.

For the whole distressed look you need to be able to sand the waxed surface to reveal the wood or another coat of paint—have a range of fine-, medium- and coarse-grade sandpapers for this purpose. I tend to find using just the fine- and medium-grades is enough, but sometimes move onto the coarser paper if I really want to distress the furniture.

The only time I use varnish is on floors, when I am doing découpage, and when I use the crackle varnish set. I prefer to apply wax to my work at the end because it has such a soft finish, can be colored and changed as you work, and stops the work chipping. Finally, have a good supply of cloths so you can wipe brushes, polish wax, apply and wipe off paint, and generally use them to clean. I use old sheets from thrift stores and charity shops and they seem to be able to provide me with an endless supply.

aging and distressing

Ways to replicate the patina of old furniture using layers of paint,
washes, wax, and working with sandpaper.

distressed pine table

USING TWO COLORS DISTRESSED

This is a simple, smooth piece of pine furniture and I felt it needed a quiet look so it could be used as a side table. I decided on Old White and Versailles since these two colors are close in tone.

My attitude to painting is to finish it quickly and get the job done, so don't mess about with little brushes. Use as big a brush as you can cope with and don't worry if the paint spreads wider than you think you want it to. When you distress pine, the unwanted color can be removed even if it does go back to the wood.

YOU WILL NEED

- Old White paint
- 1in (2.5cm) paintbrush for applying paint
- Versailles paint
- Tin of clear wax
- 2in (5cm) paintbrush for applying wax
- Cloth for removing excess wax
- Fine-grade sandpaper

Before

The table's best features are its legs so I decided to give them more focus by highlighting parts of these and the table edging.

1 Old pine that has been stripped, like this piece of furniture, can be quite a dark yellow or even orange, so it will probably need at least two coats of a light colored paint. I chose to paint the whole table in Old White first, even the parts that will later be painted in Versailles.

2 The indented legs are the highlight of the table. Using a 1in- (2.5cm-) wide brush, dab and pull the Versailles paint along the molding. Don't load the brush up with too much paint or have it too runny, otherwise it will drip. In order to achieve an even finish it's best to get the right amount of paint on each side of the leg, rather than try to do all four sides at once with the same paint load. Don't worry if some paint goes on an area you want to remain white—the paint will not be thick so you can leave it and remove it later.

3 The edges of the table top are simple, and it's tempting to use a really small brush on these narrow parts, but use a slightly larger one to speed things up.

4 Wax the table before smoothing and rubbing with sandpaper to remove some of the paint. I prefer to work by waxing a smallish but defined area, such as the edge of the table or the table top, rather than waxing the whole piece of furniture. After waxing, wipe the area with a cloth to remove any excess wax.

5 Sand the newly waxed area with a piece of fine sandpaper. Rub gently at first to see how much pressure is needed, then press harder in some areas to reveal some of the underlying wood. Although you may have decided how much to distress the piece before starting, this decision is tempered by the way the piece reacts to the paint, wax, and sandpaper. Initially I thought this would be a very lightly distressed piece, but as I worked it seemed more character would look better. Tantalizing glimpses of the wood show through in a few random areas, and the green is rubbed through to the white in places too.

TIP *Start the painting with the table turned upside down. If you paint it the right way up, then you will keep discovering bits you have missed.*

carved oak chest of drawers

USING ONE COLOR ON CARVING

I love the simple square shape of this 1930s oak chest of drawers, but I like furniture to be light and airy and wanted the interesting relief carving on the top drawer to be easily visible.

The design and shape are strong so I decided to try to bring this out by painting using just one simple color. I also wanted to highlight the carving and shape of the legs by rubbing them with sandpaper. All I had to do to prepare was to treat the plywood sides for a little woodworm damage and wipe away the cobwebs, then I was ready to paint.

Before

Oak is not a smooth wood, even when it is varnished like this chest of drawers. This means that you need to choose a technique where the paint is thick so you won't see the grain or, as I chose here, a technique where the texture of the wood is part and parcel of the gently distressed look. If you are not sure if your wood is oak, a good test is to pass your finger nail over the surface to see if you can feel the grain.

YOU WILL NEED

- Duck Egg Blue paint
- Old Ochre paint
- 2in (5cm) paintbrushes for applying paint
- Tin of clear wax
- 1in (2.5cm) paintbrush for applying wax
- Cloths for removing excess wax and polishing
- Fine- or medium-grade sandpaper

1 I chose Duck Egg Blue for the drawer interiors and Old Ochre, a pale milky caramel color, for the outside. With such dark brown wood you will need to paint two coats to fully cover both the color and the texture of the wood. On the carving I had to apply the paint with a stipple movement of the brush to make certain all the grooves, ruts, and indents were covered.

2 When the paint is dry, apply a layer of clear wax. This is best done with a large bristle brush to help reach the intricate carved areas. Wax the chest all over, wiping off any excess as you go to avoid a waxy build up.

3 For the carving take some fine- or medium-grade sandpaper and tear off a piece so you can work with it easily. Rub gently at first, then harder if necessary, to sand away the higher parts of the carving and allow the relief to show up. The sides of the chest are chamfered so I rubbed the paper along the edges here, and also along the handles, drawer fronts, and top as a way of accentuating the character of this piece of furniture. I finished off by applying another coat of wax and then polished with a cloth the next day.

The chest of drawers now looks light, fresh, and clean. The relief carving has been made more apparent by using one color and giving a gentle rub with sandpaper to reveal a little bit of the brown wood. Old Ochre is a soft antidote to the dark wood—and don't forget the surprise of the Duck Egg Blue inside the drawers.

rustic seaside chairs

USING VERY CONTRASTING COLORS

When I came across these chairs they were not particularly elegant with their short backs but I thought I could transform them into some simple seaside-inspired seating. I have chosen two rather obviously marine colors for the distressing that contrast quite a lot with each other. For this reason I have chosen to use the white on only part of the chair so it does not look too busy. I also needed to recover the seats and did so with some simple blue ticking used horizontally.

YOU WILL NEED

- Old White paint
- 2in (5cm) paintbrushes for applying paint
- Greek Blue paint
- Tin of clear wax
- 2in (5cm) paintbrush for applying wax
- Cloth for removing excess wax
- Medium-grade sandpaper

Before

These simple chairs with drop-in seats probably date from the 1940s, but they reminded me of pieces I had seen in books about old painted furniture from Sweden.

1 Apply Old White paint to the back of the chair using a dabbing motion. This will make the surface uneven once dry and give the piece a different sort of wear, making it less fussy looking. Wait for the paint to dry completely before moving on to the next step. Unfortunately, because the paint is thick, this will take a little longer than normal.

2 Take Greek Blue paint and apply it smoothly all over the chair and thinner than the first coat of white.

3 Wax all over the piece with clear wax, using a big brush to reach all the intricate details of the chair rails.

4 Wipe off the excess wax with a cloth, taking extra care to look for any build ups of wax around the vertical bars, as they can be easy to miss.

5 Rub all over the chair with medium-grade sandpaper to give it a worn look. Rub gently at first so you can gauge how much pressure you need to apply to give a worn look to the paint.

6 On the legs, rub through to the wood. Don't rub through in too many places—just a few edges, the bottom of the legs, and a little along the side. Finish with a final coat of clear wax.

TIP *When you paint a small piece of furniture with two contrasting colors like this blue and white piece, only do the two colors in one part, like the chair back for this project. Paint the rest in just one color, otherwise it will look too busy.*

rustic table

KEEPING THE GRAIN OF OLD PINE

I bought this table from an old farm that was being sold for redevelopment. It came to me covered in dirt and mess, but I could see it could be made to look terrific with a little help. I particularly like the feet—like ducks' feet—which I suppose were added so the table could be screwed to the floor for stability. The inspiration for the painting was a table I had seen in a very smart London antique shop and also a little Hungarian chair I had bought—both pieces had original, very distressed green paintwork, and the table top was natural wood.

Before

Since this table had been used as a work bench it needed a bit of work to fill in all the drill holes and make the surface reasonably smooth before painting.

TIP *When choosing the paint color, remember that it is a good idea to select a brighter color than you want to end up with because it will eventually be toned down by the dark wax. To get the heavy, textured, darkened look try to give your paintwork as much texture as you can.*

YOU WILL NEED

for the legs

- Antibes Green paint
- 2in (5cm) paintbrush for applying paint
- Tin of clear wax
- 1in (2.5cm) paintbrush for applying wax
- Cloth for removing excess wax
- Tin of dark wax
- 1in (2.5cm) paintbrush for applying dark wax
- Coarse sandpaper

for the tabletop

- Old White paint
- Water
- 2in (5cm) paintbrush for applying paint
- Cloths for removing excess paint and wax
- Tin of clear wax
- 1in (2.5cm) paintbrush for applying wax
- Tin of dark wax

1 Paint the legs and the sides of the table all over with Antibes Green. Give the paint a bit of texture by applying it thickly and unevenly. As the green is a strong color it should only need one coat, but add a second coat if necessary.

2 Apply a coat of clear wax with a brush all over the legs, wiping off any excess with a cloth.

3 Next, apply a coat of dark wax using another brush, taking care to push the wax into the texture of the paint marks. It is best to work on one area at a time, and don't allow the wax to dry before proceeding with the next step.

4 Wipe off the dark wax with a cloth. This brings out the texture of the paint since the dark wax will stay in the edges, grooves, and brush strokes. If you find the wax comes off too easily try leaving it on for a little longer before wiping it off.

5 Take some coarse sandpaper, press hard on the legs, and rub away large areas so the original color of the wood shows through obviously. Try to avoid the scratched look by applying a lot of pressure when rubbing.

6 Repeat the process of applying the dark wax, because you will have removed some of it with the sandpaper and the bare wood may need to be darkened down.

7 Make a mixture of one part Old White and one part water and paint it over the wooden table top with a brush. Keep a cloth close at hand to wipe off excess paint so the look is even and translucent.

8 Wax all over the table top using a brush and clear wax. At this stage the table top could be left with whitened or bleached looking wood.

9 I decided to make the table top darker so the contrast with the legs was not so great. To do this, I waxed the table top with a layer of dark wax. See page 47 for tips on using clear and dark wax.

10 Wipe off the excess dark wax with a cloth then apply another layer of clear wax with a brush. Wipe this off as well, which will also take off some of the dark wax. Keep applying clear wax until you have achieved your desired color for the table top. The dark wax will stay in the recesses of the wood, highlighting the grain and character.

bookcase with glass doors

USING THE WATER AND WAX METHOD

I had been looking for the opportunity to use the combination of Barcelona Orange and Olive for some time and this bookcase seemed like the ideal piece to try it out on. I painted the interior with Old Ochre to keep it light and neutral, so it would work with the strong orange and green shades of the exterior. I decided to use the water and wax method because I wanted to do something very soft and delicate that would show off the color combination.

Before
This bookcase needed just a little attention —the bottom curve had to be sawn off since half was broken, the glass replaced, and a section of wood placed down the back.

YOU WILL NEED

- Old Ochre paint
- Barcelona Orange paint
- Olive paint
- 2in (5cm) paintbrushes for applying paint
- Tin of clear wax
- Water
- 1in (2.5cm) paintbrush for applying wax and water
- Cloth for polishing

1 Start by applying a coat of Old Ochre inside and out. Once dry paint the outside in Barcelona Orange, working the brush in different directions to make the surface uneven. Some of the raised marks will show through when you start distressing the piece.

2 When the first coat is dry, paint a coat of Olive all over the exterior and leave to dry.

3 Take a brush dampened with water, put a dab of wax on it, then wipe it over the Olive paint, pressing harder in areas where you want to remove the green color, such as the corners and edges. The water in the brush will very gently take off the top layer of paint, while the wax acts to protect it.

4 Leave the bookcase overnight, then polish the paint and wax with a cloth to give the finished piece a really lovely mellow sheen.

TIP Choosing the right color combination is the most enjoyable but also the most difficult part of painting furniture. There are no hard and fast rules to follow, such as painting dark on light or cool on hot, but those principles can be a starting point. Looking for something in the room that catches the eye or will complement the finished piece, such as curtain fabrics, might also help you to make a selection.

chiffonier

VERY TEXTURED PAINT

The great thing about paint is that it can hide so much and imperfections can be made into virtues with a few simple techniques. This small late-Victorian chiffonier, a sort of slim sideboard, was in very bad condition with peeling off veneer and a missing drawer—not to mention the rickety state of the top—but I was able to save it from a sad fate by using paint! The drawer was replaced with a piece of wood, lots of glue was used for sticking down the peeling veneer and mending broken joints, and gaps were plugged with wood filler.

YOU WILL NEED

- Old White paint
- Paintbrushes in different sizes for applying paint
- Paper
- Tin of clear wax
- 1in (2.5cm) paintbrush for applying wax
- Cloths for removing excess wax and polishing
- Tin of dark wax
- White spirit
- Bowl
- 2in (5cm) paintbrush for applying white spirit mix

TIP *When painting around a mirror the best way to do it is to place a piece of paper along the inside edge, replacing the paper when one piece gets too sodden. Any paint that gets on the mirror can be removed later.*

Before

Since the piece was quite complex and almost fussy, with curves, carving, moldings, and pillars, I felt the painting should be relatively plain.

1 Begin by painting the chiffonier in Old White with a big brush, using a jabbing rather than a sweeping technique.

2 As I was using light paint on dark wood and wanted to add texture, I needed to apply three coats of Old White—leaving each to dry completely before applying the next.

3 Apply clear wax with a brush over the paint and then wipe it with a cloth to remove any excess.

4 In a bowl make a mixture of equal parts dark wax and white spirit to form a thin watery liquid.

5 Working one section at a time, apply the mixture over the white paint with a brush. Wipe off the thin mixture with a cloth so the dark color is left in the recesses and texture of the paint and the raised areas are clean.

6 In some places you might want to remove some of the dark wax mixture if the result is too dark. To do so just use a tiny amount of clear wax on your cloth and rub the wood until you are happy with the finish. See page 47 for tips on using clear and dark wax.

textured paint cabinet

DISTRESSING WITH BROWN WAX

For this project I've chosen Monet Blue, a bright Mediterranean color postioned toward the green end of the blue spectrum, which will turn a beautiful, rich, sophisticated blue with the application of the dark, tan-colored wax. To achieve a finish in this rich color you need to start with a bright paint, but bear in mind the effect that the tan wax will have on the finished piece.

YOU WILL NEED

- Monet Blue paint
- 2in (5cm) paintbrush for applying paint
- Tin of dark wax
- 1in (2.5cm) paintbrush for applying wax
- Cloth for removing excess wax
- Tin of clear wax (optional)

Before
Simple little cabinets such as this one are very adaptable, but they can look a little bland if painted too plainly. I felt it was necessary to add a splash of bright color, then tone it down slightly with the application of dark wax.

1 Paint all over the cabinet unevenly, making brush marks in all directions. Allow the paint to dry thoroughly. This may take slightly longer than usual as the paint will be thicker in some places.

2 Apply a second coat, again thickly and unevenly. It is a good idea to return to an area of paint that has begun to dry a little and make more apparent brush marks. Try stabbing the brush in just a few areas to make a different texture.

3 When the paint is thoroughly dry apply the dark wax to the whole of the chest one side at a time, making certain the brush goes in several directions to get into the texture of the paint.

TIP To achieve a good texture with your paint, allow it to thicken slightly as described on page 35. Using brush strokes in many different directions and going back over an area that has begun to dry will create additional texture. Don't worry about trying to keep the finish consistent throughout.

4 Wipe off the wax with a clean cloth quite firmly. The idea is that the dark wax stays in the textured surface of the paint. If you find that too much of the dark wax is being removed then leave it on to dry out a little more. Conversely, if too much dark wax is staying on the cabinet then use some clear wax to clean it off. If you leave the wax until it dries then it becomes difficult to remove. See page 47 for tips on using clear and dark wax.

bathroom cabinet

USING THE ORIGINAL COLOR

While I liked the shape of this piece, I felt it didn't look right or have any impact in white. To rectify this problem I decided to paint it but still incorporate some of the original white. I have chosen a darker gray and a lighter blue color to make three different tones.

Before

This is a simple little cupboard for the bathroom, which I bought already painted white.

YOU WILL NEED

- Château Grey paint
- Duck Egg Blue paint
- 2in (5cm) paintbrushes for applying paint
- Tin of clear wax
- Cloth for applying wax and polishing
- Medium- or fine-grade sandpaper

1 Paint all over the cabinet with a coat of Château Grey, working the brush in all directions and applying the paint quite thickly to give texture. Don't worry if there are any small lumps of paint, these add to the finished look.

2 When the first layer is dry, paint a second coat using Duck Egg Blue, which is medium in tone. Apply this fairly smoothly and allow to dry.

3 As this piece is quite small I applied a layer of wax with a cloth, but you can use a brush if you prefer. Wipe the wax all over the surface, then take off any excess so it doesn't feel "wet" with wax.

4 You can start sanding immediately using medium- or fine-grade sandpaper. Start sanding softly at first, then apply more pressure in places to remove the layers of blue and gray so you can see the white. Sand the whole piece, then rewax and polish.

TIP *Use the sandpaper by taking a sheet, folding it into quarters, and tearing it into four pieces. Fold a quarter in half and use that to work all over the piece. When it becomes full with paint and wax, turn it over and use the other side. When sanding the furniture take care not to rub away areas of a similar size because this can make the piece look rather spotty. It should be evenly uneven —in other words, there should be balance.*

painted Queen Anne chair

USING A KNIFE TO ADD TEXTURE TO PAINT

This Queen Anne style chair is based on furniture from the 18th century, which gained popularity because of its simple yet elegant shape. Such chairs usually have drop-in seats that can be taken out and recovered very easily. This one is based on an old Spanish painted chair I saw in a very beautiful house filled with antiques. I chose a terrific technique for this piece, but it does need a little forward planning. Make sure you have prepared the thickened paint in advance or, alternatively, this is a great way to use up paint that has thickened naturally.

Before

This type of chair can be found in nearly every second-hand furniture store as the style was popular throughout the 20th century. They are usually well made and perfect for painting, just like this example.

YOU WILL NEED

- Burgundian Red paint
- 2in (5cm) paintbrush for applying paint
- Cutlery knife
- Graphite paint
- Fine-hair artists' brush
- Tin of dark wax
- 1in (2.5cm) paintbrush for applying wax
- Tin of clear wax
- Cloth for removing excess wax and polishing
- Old White paint
- Aubusson Blue paint

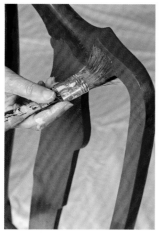

1 Paint a first coat of Burgundian Red all over the chair. If it can be removed, take away the drop-in seat before painting, otherwise cover the fabric carefully to avoid any misplaced brush strokes. Leave the paint to dry and at the same time prepare your thickened paint mixture (see tip box).

2 Take the thickened paint and apply it to the chair using a brush. Use a knife to flatten and mark the paint, giving it texture by pressing and pushing the paint around. This will give the look of many layers of old paint that have been chipped and repaired.

3 Using a reasonably long fine-hair artists' brush and Graphite paint, apply lines around the edges of the chair back and the legs. Make certain the paint is liquid enough to flow easily. Use your little finger to guide your hand but don't worry if the line is not completely perfect.

4 Add a layer of dark wax all over the chair, working the brush to reach into all the texture of the paint.

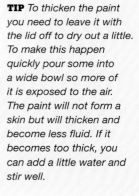

5 Wipe off the dark wax from the raised areas by applying some clear wax with a cloth and wiping it off lightly. You will notice the dark wax has stayed in the pitted areas and depressions.

6 The chair was looking rather even and dark so I decided to add some colored wax by mixing clear and dark wax with some Old White and Aubusson Blue paint on the surface of the chair. Apply a varying amount of each element to a small area at a time.

7 Work the colored wax all over the chair in stages, making some places a little more blue and others whiter by varying the amount of each paint you use. Wipe it off with a clean cloth so the lighter colour shows off the ridges of paint. Next day polish to a good sheen.

TIP *To thicken the paint you need to leave it with the lid off to dry out a little. To make this happen quickly pour some into a wide bowl so more of it is exposed to the air. The paint will not form a skin but will thicken and become less fluid. If it becomes too thick, you can add a little water and stir well.*

clouded side table

STIPPLED AND AGED TECHNIQUE

I bought a pair of modern side tables with a simple but elegant shape and have had great fun painting them to give the finished pieces quite distinct characters. This one has been treated elegantly with a mix of violet, white, and the yellowed, dusky green of Versailles used with a stippling effect. The other, the potato-print side table on page 110, is rather more playful with its spots.

Before

I found a pair of well-made and solid side tables with a very nice simple shape. The wood was dark and heavy and I thought they could do with being lightened up to make them both elegant and appealing.

YOU WILL NEED

- Versailles paint
- Old Violet paint
- Old White paint
- 2in (5cm) paintbrushes for applying paint
- Tin of clear wax
- 2in (5cm) paintbrush for applying wax
- Tin of dark wax
- Cloth for removing excess wax
- Handle (optional)

1 Paint all over the table with Versailles, the mid tone color, and leave to dry. Have ready your three tones of color, each with their own brush. I have chosen Old Violet and Old White to be the dark and light tones.

TIP *Use three colors of paint in three different tones that work well together and are not too contrasting. These could all be tones of one color or tones of different colors, as with this project. If using different colors it is better to work in fairly muted secondary or tertiary colors. Always paint the mid tone as the base color on the furniture so you can go lighter and darker with the other colors.*

2 Using two of the brushes at a time, dip them in the paint and dab all over the table. Use the darkest color the least and merge the three tones, but not quite completely, giving the paint a cloudy or dappled effect. By making the dabbing or stippling effect with the brush the paint will have an uneven texture. Apply a layer of clear wax with a brush to get into the texture and seal the paint, then work dark wax into the texture. Let the wax dry for ten minutes or so before wiping off the excess with a cloth. Finally, clean off the "top" layer with clear wax so the dark wax stays in the texture (see page 47 for tips on using clear and dark wax). I also changed the handle on the front, because I thought the metal ring didn't work well with the new color, but this is optional.

carved chair

DEALING WITH CARVING USING ONLY TWO COLORS

Whenever I see some pattern or carving on furniture I am attracted to it because it has such possibilities for painting, so this chair was a must for me. Another reason I like this piece is because a painted chair is a very easy way to add color to a room filled with neutral tones. When I had finished painting, I first tried putting clear wax on to the piece but the result was too clean looking, so I created a mix of dark and light wax instead to give it a more weathered appearance

Before

This particular chair is a bit crazy because someone has trimmed the legs, perhaps to accommodate an uneven floor, and now it is lopsided. For me though it is such quirks that add charm to a piece.

YOU WILL NEED

- Country Grey paint
- 2in (5cm) paintbrushes for applying paint
- Old Violet paint
- Tin of clear wax
- Tin of dark wax
- 1in (2.5cm) paintbrush for applying wax
- Cloth for removing excess wax and polishing
- Fine-grade sandpaper

TIP *I chose to do this piece in two colors, with the lighter coat underneath. Choosing your combination of colors is the trickiest part of an easy painting job like this. Make sure your choices are in different tones to bring out the carving well, but not so far apart in tone that it is distracting.*

1 Paint all over the chair in Country Grey, making certain you reach all the deepest parts of the carving by pushing the brush in all directions. Leave to dry. This coat will stop the wood showing through when you start using the sandpaper in step 4. Remember, painting a chair is best done by starting with it upside down.

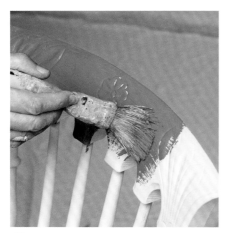

2 Paint the whole chair with a coat of Old Violet. Once that is dry, apply a second coat all over the chair to make certain all the crevices are filled.

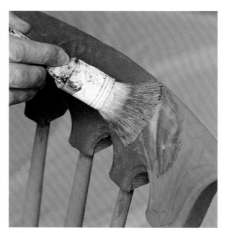

3 Make a mixture of dark wax and clear wax where the proportions are roughly 50/50. Apply a layer of wax all over the chair. I mixed the wax in small batches as I went along, so in some places the wax is a little darker than in others.

4 Wipe off any excess wax with a cloth. Take a piece of fine-grade sandpaper and rub off the top color to reveal some of the Country Grey beneath. Work gently at first to help you judge how much you want to remove.

5 To finish, apply another layer of clear and dark wax mix and polish the chair with a cloth.

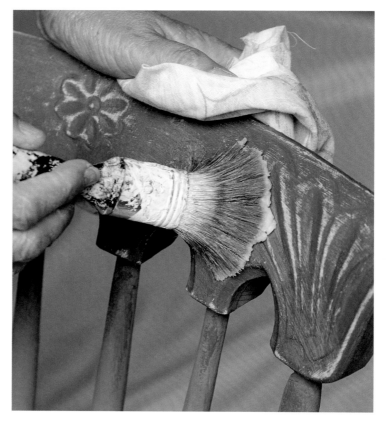

distressed ladder

WORKING WITH NEW WOOD THAT HAS KNOTS

Inspired by fruit-picking ladders, this ladder has been made from new wood to hang towels or clothes in a bathroom or bedroom. I like this one particularly because it has shaping on the rungs as if they had been already worn. You could use an old ladder here, but finding one can be difficult and a purpose-built one works just as well. It is a modern idea so I have chosen modern strong colors to reflect this.

Before
The shape of this ladder was perfect, but the color was bland and needed to be made more interesting.

YOU WILL NEED

- Knotting solution
- Cloth to apply knotting solution
- Old Violet paint
- 2in (5cm) paintbrushes for applying paint
- Emperors' Silk paint
- Tin of clear wax
- Water
- 2in (5cm) paintbrush for applying wax
- Coarse sandpaper

TIP *If you are using the ladder in a bathroom use colors that will be in contrast to the towels you use.*

1 If you are using new wood you will need to check for knots in the grain. If there are quite a few then you will need to apply knotting solution, otherwise the sap will bleed though the paint in a few months time. Luckily knotting solution is cheap, easy, and quick to use. Just dab the liquid onto a cloth and wipe over the knot. It will be dry almost immediately.

2 Paint a coat of Old Violet all over the ladder, remembering to start with it upside down first.

3 Paint over the Old Violet with Emperors' Silk, the red second coat, and leave to dry. Wipe the surface with a damp brush dipped in clear wax to take off some of the top coat of paint (see page 25, step 3). This should cause the base coat to show through, but the effect can be a bit subtle. If so, rub the ladder with a piece of coarse sandpaper as I did here to show more of the base coat.

gray and white painted chest of drawers

CHANGING THE COLOR USING WAX

I decided to make this chest look more dainty and elegant by painting the whole piece in Paris Grey, using some Old White in parts. The Paris Grey is a dignified, slightly recessive color, while Old White neatens and makes the chest look smart. I then used lots of dark wax to add shade to some areas and not so much in others . In this way the piece is split into different parts with some areas emphasized.

If you want to use this technique then look for a piece with raised moldings—and perhaps a base with a shaped and raised board—so that some parts can be picked out easily in white.

Before

This is a charming piece of furniture although it is a little crude and bulky, so I was looking for a way to paint it that would make it appear smaller and more refined.

1 Paint the whole piece of furniture with Paris Grey. You may need two coats to cover a strong color like pine.

2 Decide which areas you are going to paint with the Old White; I started on the edge of the chest first. Remember, if you are not sure you can try painting an area and if it doesn't work it can always be painted out.

YOU WILL NEED

- Paris Grey paint
- 2in (5cm) paintbrushes for applying paint
- Old White paint
- Tin of clear wax
- 2in (5cm) paintbrush for applying wax
- Tin of dark wax
- 1in (2.5cm) paintbrush for applying dark wax
- Cloth for removing excess wax and polishing

3 Move on to the edges of the drawers. If necessary apply several coats of white so that the gray can't be seen.

4 When the paint is dry, wax all over using a big brush and some clear wax. Wipe off any excess to leave a fine layer of wax. This acts as a protection for the paint and as a base for the dark layer of wax. See tip box opposite for more information on using clear and dark wax.

5 Before applying the darker layer you may need to leave the clear wax for a short time so that it is still sticky but not too damp. The wax should be wet enough to remove with a cloth but not so wet that it all comes off in one wipe. Take a smaller brush and wipe dark wax over the still damp clear wax. Work one area at a time, such as the moldings around the drawers.

6 Wipe away some of the dark wax with a cloth. You want the wood to be quite dark so you don't want to take off too much wax.

7 Apply dark wax to the center of the drawers, but this time take off more of the dark wax with the cloth. You may need to use clear wax to remove some of the color. The end result should be that the drawers are a lighter color than the rest of the chest.

TIP *Using wax well is really quite simple but you need to know what you are aiming for. Times of drying can't be given as the temperature and the absorbency of the surface affect how quickly it dries. If the wax is too dry it can't be worked and if it is too wet it is just wiped away. Don't wax the whole piece of furniture in one go because the last bit will probably be too dry before you get back to it but instead work on an area at a time, such as the side of a chest of drawers.*

Always apply clear wax first even if you know that you will apply dark afterwards. The dark wax will stain the paint if applied directly on the paint and then it is impossible to get back to the original color. With clear wax underneath, you can apply the dark wax and if it is too dark remove it with some clear wax, adjusting it until you get the right tone. The finished result of using dark wax over clear wax on light colored paint should look as if there is a discernible color difference, with some dark wax in any little niches or grooves in the paintwork or wood. The wax should not look streaked or smeared on.

distressed mirror

WORKING WITH CARVING

This is a carved pine mirror with delightful small flowers and leaves. It works well with Old White as a contrast to the wood. Paris Grey, or a very dark blue, like Aubusson Blue, are colors that would also work well with this piece, providing a cool contrast to the warm pine. If the color is too similar or too blue, it can draw attention to the orange tinge of some pine. Similar carved or molded mirrors can sometimes be found made from other materials and the same ideas about color should be taken into consideration.

WHAT YOU WILL NEED

- Old White paint
- 2in (5cm) paintbrush for applying paint
- Paper
- Coarse sandpaper

TIP *The paint does not need to be waxed because mirrors get very little handling. Also the finish needs to be as matt as possible to contrast with the mirror.*

Before

I was attracted to the floral carvings and detailing on this mirror frame and felt they would benefit from being highlighted by a little distressing.

1 Paint the mirror all over with Old White, making certain you reach into the difficult-to-reach carved intricacies. To stop the paint getting on the mirror use a piece of paper tucked into the space between the glass and the frame. Allow the paint to dry thoroughly.

2 Tear off a piece of coarse sandpaper and work it around the mirror, pressing firmly to take large parts of the paint away. If you take too much off you can always reapply the paint.

garden chair

DISTRESSING PAINT IN A NATURAL WAY

This project is slightly different to the others in this book because the effect achieved with the paint has developed naturally over several seasons in the garden. This old wooden slatted garden chair was painted several years ago and left out in the garden through all weathers—from snow to baking sun. This is not an effect that can easily be achieved without time, and is simply a matter of painting the chair in the color of your choice—Duck Egg Blue in this case—and leaving it to gradually succumb to wear. It will look good to begin with and gradually age with time. Upright areas like the back of the chair will take longer to start aging than the chair seat or a table. A garden shed, fence, or wall could also be done in the same way.

TIP *Color for the garden needs to be cool to complement the foliage and not compete with the flowers, which are mainly light, bright, and warm. The softness of Old White is good, as is Paris Grey, Country Grey, Château Grey, and the Duck Egg Blue I've chosen here. For something more contemporary Graphite and Old Violet will look stunning—these are colors that work well for both furniture and walls. If you do want to make a statement, perhaps in an urban garden, the shock of bright red such as Emperors' Silk also looks very smart on a garden bench.*

For a garden wall that acts as a backdrop and is made from wooden planks, brick, or is rendered, more natural colors like Sienna Yellow and Scandinavian Pink can be used so the wall will set off the green foliage against it. A wall that is more noticeable needs to be painted in cooler colors, so it blends with the foliage rather than standing out.

WHAT YOU WILL NEED

- Coarse sandpaper
- Duck Egg Blue paint
- 2in (5cm) paintbrush

Before

This chair was uneven in color, with the seat uncoated and the back rest in green. I liked the distressed look of the paint, but wanted it to apply to the whole piece so I decided to repaint the chair.

1 Start by removing the peeling paint and smoothing the surface with coarse sandpaper.

2 Paint the chair with a coat of Duck Egg Blue then leave to dry and let nature take its course.

working with the base

Whether the piece you want to paint is made of concrete, metal, oak, pine, or even wicker, then the paint needs to reflect and be inspired by this.

limed look oak chair

These chairs had been dipped to remove all the varnish, revealing a natural, soft brown-gray wood and allowing easier access to the hollow lines of the grain. To bring out the beautiful markings of the wood the best thing to do is fill the grain with a light color. Old White is the perfect choice because it is white without being too sharp. The finished effect looks like bleached, weather-worn wood and works well with the seaside appearance. To match this theme, I changed the seat covers to a blue and white ticking to give a more jaunty and nautical look.

Before
The markings of oak are very distinctive so when I found these old oak chairs I quickly acquired them.

YOU WILL NEED

- Old White Paint
- 2in (5cm) paintbrush for applying paint
- Water
- Sponge
- Cloths for removing excess paint and polishing
- Tin of clear wax
- 1in (2.5cm) paintbrush for applying wax

TIP *The sponge needs to be damp but not wet. As it fills up with paint you will need to rinse it out, but be sure to squeeze it almost dry before you start working on the piece again.*

1 Apply a thin coat of Old White with a firm brush to the whole chair, pushing the paint into the hollow grain of the wood. Apply the paint in different directions, even stippling in certain places to make certain the paint goes into all the hollows, before leaving to dry.

2 Take a damp sponge and wipe the paint off the piece. Although the paint is dry, the moisture on the sponge means the paint will be removed easily. Have some water near to hand so you can keep wetting the sponge.

3 In your spare hand hold a piece of dry cloth and use it to take away the now wet paint. This process keeps the paint dry in the hollows but removes it from the main surface of the wood.

4 Apply a layer of clear wax all over the surface of the chair with a brush. This will bring up the color of the wood, helping to make the contrast between the paint and the wood more apparent. Polish the surface all over with a cloth to give a smooth finish.

small oak table

BRINGING OUT THE OAK GRAIN

As soon as I saw this little oak table I thought I could really enhance it as it has so many good features. I love the markings in oak but I'd rather it was not brown, so being able to paint it and bring out the markings is very pleasing. The technique I used here is a way of achieving a limed oak look, where the niche of the grain is filled with white paint and clear wax, on a colored surface rather than on the natural oak. I chose to use Château Grey on the table, which is a shade of khaki that takes on a beautiful serenity with the white wax wash.

YOU WILL NEED

- Château Grey paint
- 1in (2.5cm) paintbrush for applying paint
- Tin of clear wax
- 1in (2.5cm) paintbrush for applying wax
- Old White paint
- Cloth for removing excess wax and paint

Before
The simple planked top combined with the shapely decorative edging made this a perfect piece for painting.

1 Start by turning the table upside down and use Château Grey to paint the whole piece; starting with it upside down will help you not to miss any parts. Because oak is a wood with a textured grain, take care to cover all the areas well with paint.

2 Using a brush apply clear wax to a small part of the table. The whole table will need to be waxed, but focus on one area at a time because the wax still needs to be wet when you apply the white paint in step 3.

3 Dip your brush in some Old White paint and work it into the clear wax— there should be equal parts wax and paint on the table. Always ensure you have clear wax on the surface before the white is added. Push your brush into the grain of the wood, working in different directions to make certain the grain is filled.

4 Wipe off the excess wax and paint as you work. Add some more clear wax if your mixture from step 3 becomes too opaque. I tend to work in small sections directly onto the piece, but you might prefer to make up a larger quantity of the wax and paint mix and work with this— just remember to apply clear wax first.

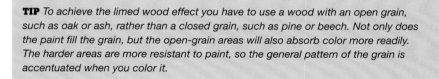

TIP *To achieve the limed wood effect you have to use a wood with an open grain, such as oak or ash, rather than a closed grain, such as pine or beech. Not only does the paint fill the grain, but the open-grain areas will also absorb color more readily. The harder areas are more resistant to paint, so the general pattern of the grain is accentuated when you color it.*

chest of drawers in a strong color

SMOOTH PAINT FOR A MODERN FINISH

The bold strong shape of this chest is perfectly suited to a modern no-frills finish. It also presents an opportunity to use a clear contemporary color rather than an antique or traditional one. I've chosen Provence blue and painted the interior of the drawers in Monet Blue. I have replaced the handles with some clear crystal ones too, and the result is a cheery but sophisticated focus for a room that is softened by cool green or cream on the wall behind.

YOU WILL NEED

- Medium-grade sandpaper
- Provence paint
- 3in (7.5cm) flat paintbrushes for applying paint
- Monet Blue paint
- Tin of clear wax
- 1in (2.5cm) brush or cloth for applying wax
- Cloth for removing excess wax and polishing
- Crystal handles

Before

I am often attracted to rather old furniture, but this chest of drawers is only a few years old and in pretty good condition, apart from the missing knobs at the top.

TIP *Using a strong color in a room can be overwhelming if the room is small and there are too many colors. Make sure you chose a strong color that is from the same part of the color palette as the soft color on the walls. A color with a bit of strength in it rather than pastels or neutrals gives life to a room.*

1 As I wanted a very smooth finish and very little distressing I sanded this piece down just a little, especially at the edges and corners, using medium-grade sandpaper.

2 Apply the Provence paint smoothly and evenly all over the chest, working the brush in the same direction as the wood grain. The paint should be smooth and flowing so add a little water to the pot to dilute if necessary. Leave the paint to dry then apply a second coat. The first coat should almost cover the color of the wood and a second coat should make the color opaque. Paint the insides of the drawers with Monet Blue.

3 Using a brush, apply a thin layer of clear wax all over the chest, including the insides of the drawers, using either a brush or a cloth, whichever is easier. A brush is best when there is intricate molding because the bristles get into the niches more easily.

4 Wipe off the excess wax using a clean fresh cloth, polishing all over as you go. For a high shine, polish the next day with a cloth.

5 To add a finishing touch to the chest, screw the clear crystal knobs into the already existing holes.

modern mahogany table

APPLYING A WASH EFFECT TO WOOD

I love the unusual shape and design of this table—the bars around the edge remind me of a classical empire piece, perhaps Swedish. I decided to bring this aspect out by painting the piece in gray blues with a wash of paint over the top, just as I have seen done with old Scandinavian tables.

YOU WILL NEED

- Coarse-grade sandpaper
- Paris Grey paint
- 2in (5cm) paintbrushes for applying paint
- Old White paint
- Versailles paint
- Cloths for wiping paint and removing excess wax
- Tin of clear wax
- 1in (2.5cm) paintbrush for applying wax
- Old Violet paint
- Tin of dark wax

Before

The seller of this table didn't know too much about its history, but it is probably fairly new and seems to be made from mahogany. It is possibly imported from Indonesia or Thailand.

TIP *The wash on this table top is a lovely effect to be used when you want to keep an interesting wood grain without it being too brown and dark. To complement the wash effect I recommend using opaque paint on the legs because walnut can be a very yellow wood and mahogany very red.*

1 Remove any varnish on the surface of the table with coarse sandpaper so that the wood is ready to take a wash.

2 Turn the piece upside down and paint the whole thing in Paris Grey, except for the table top.

3 Paint a non-diluted coat of Old White onto the surface of the table, while having a cloth ready for the next stage.

4 As soon as you have applied the paint, start wiping it off with your cloth until you are happy with the look of the wash. I found that because the mahogany is red, the effect of the Old White was to make the top slightly pink. To counteract this, once the first wash had dried I did a second wash using slightly green Versailles paint. Once the table top is dry apply a layer of clear wax with a brush. Wipe off any excess with a cloth.

5 Prepare a mix of clear and dark wax and a little Old Violet to make a colored wax. I use the lid of the wax to mix the paint and wax, mixing as I go, so the color varies. Make sure the wax is blended subtly so that it doesn't look too patchy or spotty.

6 Apply the colored wax to all of the piece apart from the table top. As the wax is mixed in batches, in some places the color is brown, while in others it is more violet. Wipe off any excess with a cloth.

wicker chair

HOW TO PAINT WICKER

Wicker chairs are readily available and are a great way to decorate a bedroom, bathroom, or to use in the garden. I find they look better with some color to them rather than in their natural state. Painting them in matt Chalk Paint® gives them a soft naturalness in keeping with the materials they are made with.

The most common way to paint these pieces is to spray them, but this is usually a very messy and smelly job. My solution is to do a simple and relaxed paint job on them, aiming not to cover every nook and cranny.

Before
Wicker chairs look lovely but they can be a bit of a trial to paint as the job can sometimes seem to be endless.

WHAT YOU WILL NEED

- Duck Egg Blue paint
- Water
- Paint tray
- 4in (10cm) paintbrush for applying paint
- Old White paint
- 1in (2.5cm) paintbrush for painting the detail

TIP *Wicker furniture just means a piece that is woven from plant material—cane, bamboo, rattan, and willow—or from twisted paper or synthetic material.*

1 Mix the Duck Egg Blue in a tray with about one third water so it is really workable and fairly sloppy.

2 Apply a coat of paint all over the chair with a brush. Use just the tip of the brush when wiping over the top of the wicker to bring out the weave rather than trying to cover the whole thing.

3 Vary the density of the application by applying more paint on areas where there is a different weave, such as along the edges.

4 This particular chair has a diamond-shaped lozenge on the back, which I have painted in Old White with a smaller brush. There is no need to varnish or wax the finished result because a matt quality is what is wanted.

ironwork lamps

DEALING WITH RUST AND PAINTING METAL

Although the rustiness of these types of lamp is often part of their charm, these pieces were just plain dirty and needed work—but I still wanted to retain the aged vintage look. The usual thing to do is to cover rust with paint to stop it spreading, but this would make them look characterless and new, definitely not an effect I like. My method is really just a patch up and it is probably not the best long-term solution. However, I find it seals the rust and by keeping it inside it will slow down the corrosion of the metal. I've kept one of the stands as a lamp but the other one I converted back to a romantic candle holder.

Before

I found these two romantic-looking ironwork lamp stands, with their lovely scroll work, in someone's shed. One of them was particularly lovely, with a wrought iron barley twist stand. They were painted white but had started to rust.

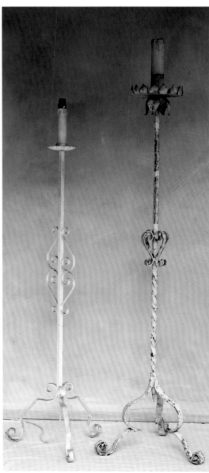

YOU WILL NEED

- Coarse sandpaper
- Old White paint
- 2in (5cm) paintbrush for applying paint
- Cloth for removing excess paint
- Tin of clear wax (optional)
- 1in (2.5cm) paintbrush for applying wax (optional)

1 Use some coarse sandpaper to rub the surface of the metal down, getting rid of any loose paint and rust.

2 Apply Old White to the lamp, working on one defined area at a time rather than applying all the paint in one go. Once the section you are focusing on is finished, move on to the next step while the paint is still wet.

3 Wipe off the paint with a cloth to leave a film of white. This will allow the imperfections to show but they will not be quite as obvious. Repeat for the rest of the lamp. Once the whole lamp has been painted you can leave it as it is or alternatively apply a coat of clear wax with a brush to help seal the surface.

TIP *If you find a metal lamp painted black, as many are, then try the same technique using Graphite.*

French workman's shelf

REVEALING THE GRAIN OF THE WOOD

This is a copy of shelves that can often be found in the flea markets, or "brocantes," of France. Originally they were a working man's simple open wardrobe with a shelf for hats and pegs and a rail for hanging clothes. Now they are used not only in the bedroom, but also in the hallway, the bathroom, and even the kitchen. There are a number of ways that this one could be painted, but I decided to use the fact that it is new smooth wood and show a little of it.

YOU WILL NEED

- Paris Grey paint
- 2in (5cm) paintbrush for applying paint
- Fine-grade sandpaper
- Tin of clear wax
- 1in (2.5cm) paintbrush for applying wax
- Cloth for removing excess wax

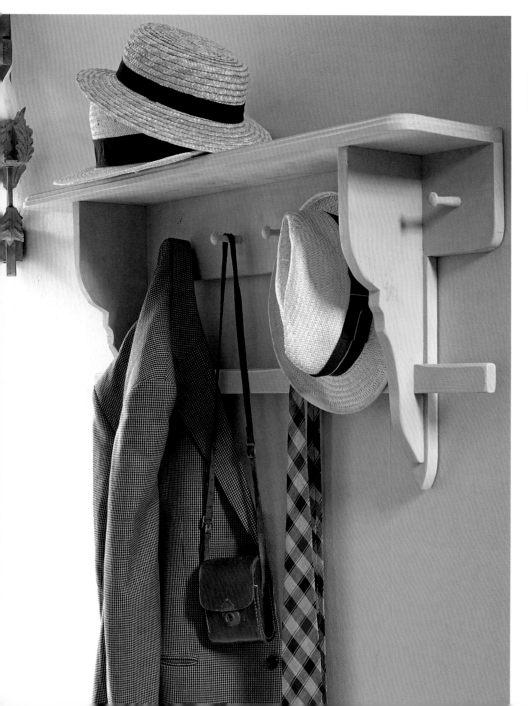

Before

This shelf had a lovely wood grain that I felt should be on show and not covered with too much paint.

TIP *New pine wood is pale and warm—although it will darken with time—so bear this in mind when you choose a paint color. On this surface a cooler color will probably give a better result than a much warmer one.*

1 Apply a thin coat of Paris Grey paint evenly on the shelf going in the same direction as the wood grain. Leave to dry. When the wood is waxed the paint will become slightly translucent allowing you to see the grain.

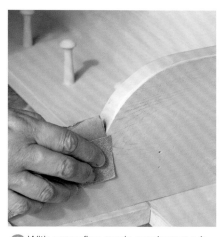

2 With some fine-grade sandpaper rub down parts of the shelf, focusing on areas that can be easily seen or where the wood grain is more apparent. Rub smoothly all over to make the wood and paint very flat.

3 Work some clear wax into the paint with a brush to achieve a thin even layer. You could use a cloth here but a brush is better because it will allow you to reach the most inaccessible areas more easily.

4 Wipe the piece gently with a cloth to leave a smooth layer of wax all over and to bring out the grain of the wood. Depending on the thickness of the paint the grain will be more visible in some areas than others.

5 Finally, rub the whole shelf with the sandpaper to give a really smooth and flat finish. At this stage you could also take more of the paint off if you feel that not enough wood is showing. Finish with a final thin coat of wax.

washed pine bookcase

DEALING WITH ORANGE PINE

Some people hate the idea of losing the wood grain when you paint, so I have used a wash of color on this bookcase. To make the piece more interesting I have given it a look inspired by a side table I saw in a French antiques shop, which had inlaid wood to create the striped drawer front. To replicate the texture of inlaid wood I have softened the edges of the masking tape by tearing them.

Before
This is a very useful small bookcase but without much character—and the color is very orange, like all modern pine, and out of keeping with a modern interior.

WHAT YOU WILL NEED

- Country Grey paint
- Paint tray
- 2in (5cm) paintbrush
- Cloth for removing excess paint
- Masking tape
- Tin of dark wax
- Tin of clear wax
- 1in (2.5cm) paintbrush for applying wax
- Cloths for removing excess wax and polishing

TIP *Use only neutral colors to dull down pine as any additional color may highlight the orange. I have used Country Grey for my wash as the putty tone dulls down the color of the wood.*

1 Pour out some Country Grey paint into a container and set aside to dry slightly, ready for use in step 5. See tip box on page 35 for details of how to thicken the paint. With the remaining Country Grey, paint the bookcase one side at a time. While the paint is still wet move on to the next step.

2 Wipe the wet paint with a cloth so the paint is even but dispersed and the wood grain is visible. Remember that the wax can cause the paint to become a little more transparent, so leave the paint slightly more opaque at this stage than you want the finished coat to be.

3 For the drawer front, take small pieces of masking tape and tear them carefully down the center so that each strip will have a torn edge and a straight edge.

4 Stick two pieces of masking tape onto the drawer front, butting straight edge to straight edge, to create a stripe with uneven sides running vertically down the drawer. Leave a gap and repeat, to give a series of uneven and rough edge stripes.

5 Paint the drawer front with the Country Grey, but this time using the paint you set aside to dry in step 1. Make sure there is good opaque coverage across the whole front.

6 Once the paint has dried, remove the masking tape carefully to leave a series of stripes on the drawer.

7 Prepare a mixture of one part clear and one part dark wax.

8 Apply a thin layer of wax with a brush all over the piece to give it a warm, knocked-back look. Wipe off the excess with a cloth.

candelabra

WORKING WITH BRASS

I found the shape of this piece, with its twisted flowing arms, particularly
inspiring and I knew it could easily be restored to its former glory. By painting
it in Graphite, the candelabra takes on a baroque look that gives it more
weight and presence.

YOU WILL NEED

● Graphite paint

● 2in (5cm) paintbrush for applying paint

● Tin of dark wax

● 1in (2.5cm) paintbrush for applying wax

● Cloth for removing excess wax

● Fine-grade sandpaper

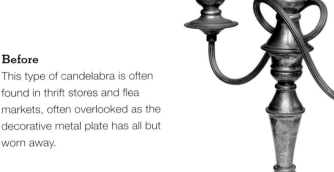

Before

This type of candelabra is often found in thrift stores and flea markets, often overlooked as the decorative metal plate has all but worn away.

1 Old candlesticks often have dry, dripped wax on them that needs to be removed. The best way to do so is by painting the area where the candles go first to show up the wax, then scrape it off. Then paint all over the rest of the piece with Graphite, turning the candelabra upside down and starting at the base first.

2 When the dark gray Graphite is dry, take a well-charged brush of dark wax, and apply all over. The wax will darken the color of the paint to a soft black.

3 Wipe off the excess wax with a cloth then gently sand some parts of the candlestick, such as the edges with decorative molding, so the brass shows through. Polish with the cloth to achieve a soft sheen.

TIP *Chalk Paint® can be used on a variety of metal items, including brass candlesticks or silver chandeliers, and wiping away the black to reveal a little of the gilt always looks very elegant.*

staircase

PAINTING AND VARNISHING A WOODEN FLOOR

Painting a whole staircase is a quick, practical, and economical solution to camouflaging a new step added to an existing staircase, and also allows you to add some extra color to the area. Adding a coat of paint to the stairs opens up many possibilities—from highlighting the edging, as I have done, to applying vertical stripes, painting the steps a different color to the risers, or simply using one bold color.

YOU WILL NEED

- Château Grey paint
- 2in (5cm) paintbrushes for applying paint
- Paint trays
- Scandinavian Pink paint
- Extra-strong semi-matt lacquer
- 4in (10cm) brush for lacquer

TIP *If your floorboards are in good enough condition you could apply the paint thinly as a wash, painting it on and wiping it off if you want a slightly more opaque effect. The same application of lacquer would follow.*

Before
I had to add an extra step to the rather worn existing staircase in my Victorian home when we built our new garden room, and it required a coat of paint.

1 I have chosen two colors that work well together, Scandinavian Pink for the edging and Château Grey for the rest. Simply paint the whole staircase first with the gray, then once it is dry paint the edging in the pink.

2 When all the paint is dry, varnish the staircase with a strong lacquer. I have used a water-based semi-matt product.

garden planter

PAINTING CEMENT TO LOOK LIKE LEAD

I considered painting this planter with a wash of Old White but because it was so classic in shape I felt it needed to be a little more traditional. I decided the best option was to make it look as though it was made of lead. This is simply done using Graphite and rubbing with fine sandpaper. Where there is a straight ridge the fine sandpaper smooths the paint and makes it look silvery gray, rather like pencil marks. This is in contrast to the matt paintwork and it is this subtle contrast that creates the effect.

YOU WILL NEED

- Graphite paint
- 2in (5cm) paintbrush
- Fine-grade sandpaper

Before
I found a pair of particularly shapely cement planters but wanted to make them a bit special.

TIP *I have left this pot out in torrential rain and the finish stayed the same, but I have not tested it for a long period of time. It could be used inside as a planter, or the same technique could be used on other pieces of carved furniture.*

1 Brush all over the planter with Graphite paint and leave to dry. Apply a second coat to make certain you have covered everywhere including all the little nooks and crannies.

2 With fine-grade sandpaper rub all over the paintwork, or at least the raised molded parts. Here the top edges, which are long and uninterrupted, were rubbed finely to make them smooth and give them a slight sheen, like the finish on the cow parsley chest of drawers (see page 118). Stop sanding when you are satisfied with the look. There will be two different-colored grays; the lighter shade will be very smooth with a lovely sheen.

using color

Color combinations are the single most important aspect to painting furniture. Here are techniques and guidelines on how to use color and tone to achieve the effect you want.

painting and waxing a wall

ADDING TEXTURE TO A FLAT WALL

I wanted to give this wall a really smart polished look, but with a little texture in the paint so that it didn't look too flat. Graphite paint looks very good with the white plaster statue against it and certainly makes a great statement. In contrast, Old White with clear wax also looks very appealing as a polished wall. A stronger color with clear and dark wax could also look good.

Before
This wall was very smooth because it was relatively new plaster that had received just one application of paint.

YOU WILL NEED

● Graphite paint
● Sponge roller and paint tray
● Tin of clear wax
● Cloth or 2in (5cm) paintbrush for applying wax
● Cloth for polishing

TIP *If you have a really large area to paint and wax you might find the polishing is best done with an electric buffer.*

1 Apply two coats of Graphite paint using a sponge roller. Have some solid areas of paint but don't try to make the whole wall completely opaque. Avoid creating a pattern or texture as this can become too busy. Remember that when you apply the clear wax any pattern will become much more apparent.

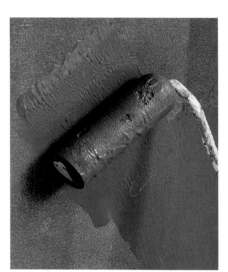

2 Using a cloth or a large brush apply lots of clear wax to the wall. Spread the wax all over the surface to create a thin layer— there shouldn't be any excess because it will be worked over the whole wall. Don't leave any thick areas of wax as this might dry white. Polish the next day— this is easier on the second day—for a really good sheen.

polished plaster

MAKING A ROUGH WALL SMOOTH WITH CHARACTER

I wanted to give this wall color, depth, and interest. The finished result has little flecks of white from the base color, as well as touches of Sienna Yellow and Old Ochre, but still looks and feels very smooth. There are many color options for this technique, such as Burgundian Red under Sienna Yellow, with small patches of deep red coming through.

Before
My kitchen wall was painted in white and was rough, with uneven and pitted plaster in some places.

WHAT YOU WILL NEED

- Sienna Yellow paint
- Woolen roller and paint tray
- Old Ochre paint
- Water
- 4in (10cm) paintbrush
- Cloths for removing excess paint and wax
- Tin of clear wax
- 2in (5cm) paintbrush for applying wax
- Fine- or medium-grade sandpaper

1 Apply the Sienna Yellow using a woolen roller so that the paint is rough and textured. Don't roll out too far because this can make the paint too smooth.

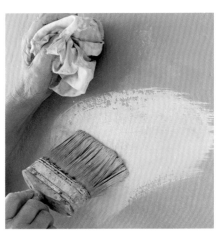

2 Once the first coat is dry, apply a wash using Old Ochre diluted 50/50 with water. Take a large brush in one hand and paint the wall with the Old Ochre mix. With the other hand, use a cloth to spread the paint thinly and mute the Sienna Yellow underneath. Allow the paint to dry for half an hour or so—a few damp spots can make interesting marks.

3 Paint a layer of clear wax on the wall using a brush and then wipe off any excess with a cloth.

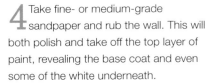

4 Take fine- or medium-grade sandpaper and rub the wall. This will both polish and take off the top layer of paint, revealing the base coat and even some of the white underneath.

TIPS *If you want to create this finish on a very large area then you might find an electric sander cuts down the work. Wait until the wax is completely dry before sanding as it can clog up the sandpaper very quickly when still soft.*

patchwork drawers

MAKING BRIGHT COLORS WORK
TOGETHER

To make lots of colors work together
without the end result looking too
garish, choose ones that are roughly in
the same tone band. That way you can
avoid one color being much lighter than
the others. For my chest I have chosen
mainly cool shades, but with warm
colors for the top two drawers. The
deeper tone of the framework will help
to soften the brightness of the drawers.

Before
I had been looking for a tall chest of
drawers that would give me the opportunity
to paint the drawer fronts in a rainbow of
colors. When I saw this piece I knew it
would be perfect.

YOU WILL NEED

- Burgundian Red paint
- Emperors' Silk paint
- Old Violet paint
- Greek Blue paint
- Monet Blue paint
- Aubusson Blue paint
- Provence paint
- Antibes Green paint
- 2in (5cm) paintbrush
- Tin of clear wax
- 1in (2.5cm) paintbrush for applying wax
- Cloth for polishing

TIP *If you want the colors to look more vibrant, choose a very light color for the framework. Avoid using white because unless the wall that the chest stands against is a strong color, the framework would not "hold" the colors. Instead try using a pastel color such as Duck Egg Blue. A darker paint does help to contain the colors, although something like Graphite would be much too stark.*

1 Before you begin, plan the colors and their order on the drawers. After choosing my seven colors I arranged the pots in order, moving them around until I was satisfied. I decided on a very logical order, which is the hot reds first, then the blues with the most red in them, the Old Violet and the Greek Blue following, then the blues moving toward green, and ending with the final drawer painted in Antibes Green, a bright Mediterranean color.

2 Take out all the drawers and start painting the framework of the chest in a strong color; I chose Aubusson Blue. This is cool, like most of the other colors, so will absorb their brightness—but is slightly deeper in tone so it frames and contains them.

3 Paint each of the drawer fronts with two coats of your chosen color. Pick one of the brighter colors to use for the interiors of the drawers.

4 Apply a layer of clear wax all over the chest, including the insides of the drawers. Finish by polishing with a cloth.

pastel chest of drawers

COMBINING COLORS TO PULL A PIECE TOGETHER

This chest lent itself perfectly to painting in a delicate palette of pastel colors, using Paris Grey as a base coat to unite them all. The beading around the drawers creates a clear border so this is a good piece for painting. If you prefer stronger colors, see the patchwork drawers on page 86. When choosing your colors, look at other furniture and fabrics in the room for inspiration.

Before

I chose this piece because it is well put together and a good shape that is ideal for experimenting on.

TIP *Paint is to a certain extent translucent so the underneath color will change the top coat. For instance, if you paint red on one drawer and blue on another, then paint them both in the same neutral color, the neutral color will look different depending on the base coat.*

YOU WILL NEED

- Fine-grade sandpaper
- Paris Grey paint
- 2in (5cm) paintbrushes for applying paint
- Versailles paint
- Duck Egg Blue paint
- Louis Blue paint
- Tin of clear wax
- 1in (2.5cm) paintbrush for applying wax
- Cloth for polishing

1 I started by sanding the piece quite lightly, especially on the edges and corners, as the finish was a little bit shiny and I was certain I did not want any of the orange color of the wood coming through. I then painted the whole piece in Paris Grey, including the handles as these should not be apparent and get in the way of the colors.

2 Pick colors that are similar in tone both to each other and to the Paris Grey base—I chose Versailles, Duck Egg Blue, and Louis Blue. All are not only similar in tone but also occupy the same cool part of the color wheel—Versailles and Louis are furthest apart.

3 Paint each drawer front in a color using any combination you like. I divided the blues and had the greener color on two drawers. Apply a layer of clear wax with a brush and then buff it up afterwards using a cloth to remove some of the wax. For this piece I felt the emphasis should be on the colors rather than the finish.

side table in oriental colors

USING WAX TO THIN THE TOP COAT OF PAINT

The rich reds, browns, and blacks of Chinese painted and lacquered furniture are so inspiring and I often look for pieces on which I can achieve this look. Apart from the color, the distinctive thing about this finish is the sheen, which is unlike traditional European finishes. It is not hard and glossy, but has a soft high sheen that is best achieved with a lot of wax and elbow grease. Or you could cheat and use an electric buffer instead!

YOU WILL NEED

- Emperors' Silk paint
- 2in (5cm) paintbrushes for applying paint
- Graphite paint
- Tin of clear wax
- 1in (2.5cm) paintbrush for applying wax
- Cloth for removing excess wax and polishing
- Fine-grade sandpaper

Before
I found this very unusual low side table and thought it had a faintly oriental look with its square shape, angled sides, and proportions that are not in the European tradition.

1 Paint all over the table with Emperors' Silk paint, including the inside of the drawer. This color is a pure red so you will find that it needs several coats to cover the wood. The reason for this is that reds are notoriously lacking in opacity, especially when painted over oak, which has a lot of texture.

2 Once the paint is dry, apply a single even coat of Graphite. Don't have the paint too thick and don't paint the inside of the drawer. The idea is that the paint will be thin enough to cover the table completely but the red will still show through. Don't worry if the red is more visible in some place than others, just try to avoid brush marks.

3 Once the paint is dry, wax the whole table with a brush one side at a time. You will notice that the wax makes the thin coat of Graphite slightly transparent and the red will make it appear slightly brown.

4 Wipe away the excess wax with a cloth, rubbing quite hard to see if you can take off any Graphite paint to add to the distressed look.

5 Use a little fine-grade sandpaper and work it gently on the surface, taking off some of the Graphite to expose the bright red of the Emperors' Silk underneath. Polish well, especially the next day, to get a high shine.

Swedish-colored dresser

MIXING PAINT ON A SMALL SIDE TABLE

The dresser that this project is based on was finished just in white and deep blue, and the decoration consisted of very loosely painted moldings with some handpainted figures. I thought I would recreate this from memory but without the figures. The particular aspect of this piece of furniture that I liked was the loose style of brushstrokes and the specific Swedish blue that had been used with the Old White.

YOU WILL NEED

- Old White paint
- Aubusson Blue paint
- 1in (2.5cm) paintbrush for applying paint
- Tin of clear wax
- Tin of dark wax
- 1in (2.5cm) paintbrush for applying wax
- Cloth for removing excess wax

TIP *To achieve the Swedish look the right colors need to be used. Aubusson Blue is a particularly Swedish-style shade—it is based on Prussian Blue, a color that was discovered in the 18th century and became available to all. Other Swedish-style colors include Château Grey, a natural brownish-green, Scandinavian Pink, an earthy natural brown pink, and ochers such as Sienna Yellow.*

Before

It was something about the raised back with its oval on this small side table that reminded me of a beautiful old painted dresser I saw in a book about painted 18th-century houses in Sweden.

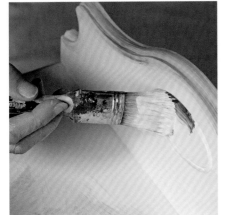

1 The trick to painting this piece in a loose way is to add a little blue onto the side of a paintbrush that is already loaded with Old White (see page 97). Use the brush to coat the moldings with blue, but allow some blue to spread onto the main parts of the furniture where it can be blurred and blended into the white.

2 I painted the whole table, giving the central oval shape emphasis by working the blue into the molding. Allow the blue to make a gentle "blush" in and around the middle of the oval. I applied clear then dark wax to the whole table with a brush, again emphasizing the oval shape by filling the molding with dark wax. Remove any excess wax with a cloth.

distressed cupboard

MIXING PAINT DIRECTLY ON FURNITURE AND COLORING WAX WITH PAINT

I have noticed that on old painted furniture the color of the paintwork is not always as even as might be expected. I suppose this is because parts have been repainted or have faded over the years. I wanted to recreate this look in my painting of this large pine cupboard.

Before
This pine cupboard was very large and looked a little uninteresting. It needed some textured paintwork to avoid appearing too flat.

WHAT YOU WILL NEED

- Château Grey paint
- Old White paint
- 2 paint trays
- 4in (10cm) paintbrush for applying paint
- 1in (2.5cm) paintbrush for adding detail
- Tin of clear wax
- 1in (2.5cm) paintbrush for applying wax
- Cloths for removing excess wax
- Primer Red paint
- Tin of dark wax
- Medium-grade sandpaper

TIP *I chose Château Grey as my main color to which I added various amounts of Old White, but you could easily reverse the two and have Old White as the main color.*

1 After deciding on your two colors, fill two trays with the paints in about equal measures. Have a large brush and a smaller brush ready.

2 Take the large brush first and dip one corner into one tray of paint. Repeat with the other corner and the second tray so that you have equal amounts of paint on each end.

3 Tip the brush to the Château Grey side to begin with and apply the paint to the inset strips, then tip the brush to the other side to apply more of the white to the paneled area.

4 Having started off with about equal amounts on each corner, start to take more of the darker Château Grey on the brush and continue to paint the piece. Add more of the lighter Old White on the brush and wipe the paint over the panels to make them a little lighter.

5 Use the small and the large brush to make various marks with both paints. Try not to worry if they are a bit obvious as they will be toned down later with wax and sandpaper. These marks should not be evenly placed all over, just on part of the cupboard. Blend and merge the paint together on the rest of the cupboard so the color varies, but keep it subtle. Use the small brush to reach difficult areas and to make smaller marks than the larger brush.

6 Paint the inside of the cupboard and drawer with Primer Red. Don't worry if it slightly bleeds through to the front of the cupboard, as it does around the top of the doors and near the hinges (opposite), because this helps to give patina and interest. Apply clear wax to one cupboard door at a time and then wipe lightly with a cloth so the wax isn't too wet.

7 While the clear wax is still sticky, start applying the dark wax in places. Wipe it with a cloth as you go so you don't make it too dark and patchy.

8 Now apply just a little of the Old White paint to the wax. Too much and it won't mix; too little and the wax will have no color. Spread the paint and wax mixture all over the piece in stages, concentrating on areas of dark wax. Wipe with a cloth and add more clear wax if necessary until you are satisfied with the look. The "white wax" will go into the brush marks and pitted parts of the brushwork, and soften the color of the dark wax.

9 Use sandpaper lightly to help polish and smooth out the surface of the cupboard.

Venetian-inspired cupboard

USING 18TH-CENTURY COLORS

This piece is fairly simple but it does have nicely shaped door panels and there is a gentle curve along the front that gives it some elegance. The colors I have used are Old White, Duck Egg Blue, and Primer Red, but instead of painting them flat I have made the blue lighter in some places. To do this add a little Old White by dipping the end of the brush into the paint and then merging the two colors on the piece of furniture (see page 97).

Before
This cupboard had been in my living room in its original white state for some time, waiting for inspiration. Finally, the idea came to paint it in the colors of a favorite piece of 18th-century Venetian furniture.

YOU WILL NEED

- Duck Egg Blue paint
- Old White paint
- 2in (5cm) paintbrush for applying paint
- Primer Red paint
- Small soft bristle artists' brush for panel edges
- Medium- and fine-grade sandpaper
- Tin of clear wax
- 1in (2.5cm) paintbrush for applying wax
- Tin of dark wax
- Cloth for polishing

1 I painted the main part of the cupboard in Duck Egg Blue. Vary the color by dipping a corner of the brush into the Old White and applying it onto the blue, causing the colors to almost merge. The finish will be uneven all over—very light in some places and darker in others. Apply a coat of Old White to the panels, having taken the lid off the night before to allow the paint to thicken and give it texture (see tip box on page 35).

2 I painted the inside of the cupboard, the cornice, and the edges of the inner panel in Primer Red to help define the shape of the cupboard, as on the original piece I was influenced by. To keep the finish neat on the panels you need to use a small brush. Don't worry too much if paint goes over the edges as this helps to make it appear more handpainted, and any excess can be rubbed away with sandpaper.

3 Apply a coat of clear wax all over the painted areas with a brush. Add some dark wax to a few places to deepen the shade in certain parts of the cupboard. Next, make a mix of one part clear wax and one part Old White to form a colored wax (see step 8, page 98). Put a layer of this mixture on the surface with a brush to soften the piece and lighten areas that look too dirty. Rub the surface lightly with sandpaper and finish by adding a final coat of clear wax.

TIP *The hinges on the cupboard were black and particularly unattractive. Like all my pieces I usually just paint over all handles and hinges and then wax them. Some of the paint does come off but this is better than seeing bare metalwork glaring at you.*

painted floor

USING A SPONGE TO PRINT SQUARES

The original paint on my kitchen floor was starting to wear away and the concrete underneath began to show through. Rather than simply apply one color I wanted to try something new to give the floor a more interesting look. I decided to go for a rustic approach, selecting gray as my base coat and then applying squares of buttery Cream and Old White quickly and simply with a square sponge.

YOU WILL NEED

- Paint tray and roller
- Masking tape and string
- Paris Grey paint
- Old White paint
- Cream paint
- Square sponge
- 2in (5cm) paintbrush
- Clear, extra strong varnish

1 Use a roller to cover the floor with the base gray color. Make sure you have vacuumed the floor before you start to avoid any unwanted detritus when you apply the paint.

2 Starting in the center of the room, tape a piece of string to the floor from one side of the room to the other. Spread the Old White evenly in the paint tray. Dip the square sponge into the tray, making sure it is wholly covered, and press onto the floor at regular intervals, using the string as a guide. Repeat on the other side of the string. When you have done two lines of squares, move the string for the next two lines and continue until the whole room is done.

3 Go over some of the squares you have already made with a third color. Print some next to each other and leave gaps in other areas. The sponge will cover the squares unevenly so some of the white will show, but it is this randomness that looks so appealing.

4 Give the floor two coats of extra strong varnish, using a brush at the edges and a roller over the rest.

handpainting

Don't be intimidated by the idea of handpainting. You don't have to have drawing ability to apply hand-drawn and painted decoration to your furniture. Just enjoy by doodling with the end of your brush into wet paint, or print with potatoes or the edge of card, for instance.

elegant chair legs

MAKING LINES TO EMPHASIZE CURVES

I bought this delightfully elegant set of four chairs, with their shapely backs and simplified cabriole legs, from a friend who was moving house. I chose a neutral color to work with the gold fabric and defined the leg curve with a line of Olive paint. I also replaced the original braid with blue ribbon, aiming to make the finished chairs very smart.

Before

YOU WILL NEED

- Scissors
- Paris Grey paint
- 2in (5cm) paintbrush for applying paint
- Olive Green paint
- Small artists' brush for applying lines
- Tin of clear wax
- 1in (2.5cm) paintbrush for applying wax
- Cloth for polishing
- Measuring tape
- ½in (1cm) wide ribbon
- Fabric glue

1 Remove the gold braid from the edge of the chair so that you can paint right up to the fabric edge. This is easily done as the braid is fixed in place with only glue.

2 Paint the chair smoothly all over with Paris Grey, taking care not to get any on the fabric.

3 The chair has a simplified cabriole shape that I have highlighted at the top by painting a thin line of Olive Green along the edge with an artists' brush. You might want to lightly draw the line first with a pencil before painting to avoid mistakes. Repeat on the other front leg, painting a line on both edges of each leg.

4 Apply a layer of clear wax all over the legs using a brush. With a cloth rub gently on the olive edges. This will remove some of the paint and help to soften the hardness of the line.

5 Measure around the base of the seat. Cut a slightly longer length of ribbon as there needs to be an overlap at the back of the chair. Apply fabric glue around the base of the seat and carefully fix the ribbon in place.

TIP *Characterless brown varnished wood on the legs of upholstered chairs does not usually bring out the best in a fabric's texture, color, or pattern. If the chair is undistinguished with a patterned fabric, pick a color from the fabric and use it to paint the legs. Alternatively, try applying a color with impact to make the chair more appealing, like a red or a strong green.*

shelves with spots

HOW TO DO HANDPAINTING

There is something charming about a homemade piece like these shelves and although slightly damaged, they are perfect for painting. The edges were probably cut with a jigsaw and the patterns made by drilling holes in the side, creating a piece that was aching for some decorative painting. It is often quite difficult to make shelves look interesting since there is little to see, but dots, lines, and spots are quite achievable, even for an amateur with little experience.

Before
This attractive decorative shelving unit was unfortunately ruined because the bottom shelf was badly warped, probably through exposure to water or heat.

YOU WILL NEED

- Country Grey paint
- 2in (5cm) paintbrush for applying paint
- Scandinavian Pink paint
- Small artists' brush
- Water
- Tin of clear wax
- 1in (2.5cm) paintbrush for applying wax
- Cloth for removing excess wax

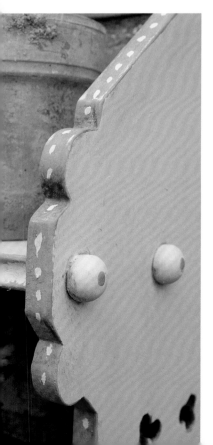

1 Paint the whole piece with Country Grey and allow to dry. You will probably need two coats as the brown wood underneath is quite dark.

2 Where and how you paint the lines and spots depends a lot on the shelves you find. These shelves had a molding with a groove in it, so I simply pressed lightly with the side of the brush and ran it along the raised edges.

3 Mix a small amount of clean water with the Scandinavian Pink to make the paint fluid, but not so that the mixture drips. Add a few drops to begin with, then some more if necessary to achieve the right consistency. Along the wavy edge of the bottom shelf I made a series of dots, and then added other spots to the rest of the shelves. Apply a layer of clear wax with a brush to protect and finish off the piece. Remove any excess wax with a cloth.

TIP *Choosing a brush for the painting of fine dots and lines is important. This doesn't mean you have to go out and buy an expensive sable hair brush, but you should avoid a very cheap child's brush as they have no "spring" in the hairs. Find a brush that has a bit of spring and comes to a reasonable point. Press the end of the brush—it should resist a little, and the hairs should return quickly back to their original position.*

potato-print side table

ADDING SIMPLE DECORATIVE TOUCHES

For this side table I wanted to do something with spots and one of the easiest ways to do this is with potato printing. A polka dot design can look very childlike, but by choosing a smart gray with white spots the finished result is charming and sophisticated. For the drawer interiors I chose a splash of a strong green, but you could try a softer color that will work well with your interior instead.

Before

I found a pair of well-made and solid side tables with a very nice, simple shape. The wood was dark and heavy and I thought they could do with being lightened up to make them both elegant and appealing. See page 36 for an alternative idea.

YOU WILL NEED

- Paris Grey paint
- 1in (2.5cm) paintbrushes for applying paint
- Antibes Green paint
- Potato
- Non-serrated knife
- Felt-tip pen
- Cloth
- Old White paint
- Scrap paper
- Tin of clear wax
- 2in (5cm) paintbrush for applying wax
- Fine-grade sand paper

1 Paint the outside with the Paris Grey, including the uppermost edges of the drawer and the metal drawer pull. Next, paint the interior of the drawer with one coat of Antibes Green.

2 Cut a potato in half with a non-serrated knife. Draw a circle on the cut side with a felt-tip pen either freehand or using a coin as a template. Some potatoes can be very wet inside so dab the cut end with a cloth to absorb the moisture before you start drawing.

3 Using the pen line as a guide, push the knife about ½in (1.5cm) down into the potato and cut around the sides of the circle.

4 Next, cut into the side of the potato until you reach the point where you cut down into the circle in the previous step. Slice away bits from the side of the potato to form a raised circle that will be used as a spot stamp. Alternatively, rather than cutting a shape into a potato you could use a smaller round potato cut in half, or maybe even try a carrot!

5 Test your stamp by dabbing some white paint onto the potato circle with a brush and pressing it on some scrap paper. The spots formed may be a little uneven the first few times, so it is best to practice until you work out the correct amount of paint and pressure needed.

6 When you are happy with your practice spots, start printing them on the table. I have applied mine randomly, starting where I knew I wanted one and then leaving a comfortable gap between that and the next one.

7 Once I had finished with the potato I painted the molding around the top Old White to give the piece a neat edging. This helps to offset the randomness of the spots.

8 Using a big brush, apply a thin layer of clear wax all over the table including the drawer handle.

9 Rub the handle lightly with the sandpaper so that just a little of the metal shows through.

TIP *Printing with a potato will always give you an uneven finish so don't be disappointed if the spots are not smooth and uniform. If you want your spots to look flat and identical then you will need to do them with a stencil.*

Victorian table

TWO WAYS TO MAKE LINES

Recently I remembered the Victorian fashion for painting lines to embellish furniture in a very gentle and underplayed way. These would have been painted by hand, but this is a difficult skill to master. I have developed a great technique for achieving something that imitates the uneveness of old painted furniture, by using masking tape. I have also done some handpainted lines on the drawer using a small brush. The furniture is old and uneven and, of course, that is its charm, so the masking tape lines must be made a little random and uneven, too.

YOU WILL NEED

- Duck Egg Blue Paint
- 2in (5cm) paintbrush for applying paint
- 1in (2.5cm) wide masking tape
- Small scissors
- Old White paint
- Water
- Small long-haired artists' brush
- Tin of clear wax
- 1in (2.5cm) paintbrush for applying wax
- Cloth for buffing

TIP *Masking tape is naturally bendy so it is easy to make uneven lines of varying widths. This is important as in these days of factory-made perfection we have forgotten the warmth of characterful handmade furniture. When you remove the tape a little bit of paint comes off, which helps towards creating the distressed look. The longer you leave the tape on, the more paint will be removed.*

1 Paint the whole table with a coat of Duck Egg Blue and leave to dry. Mark out a rectangle about 1in (2.5cm) from the edge of the table top using the masking tape. Don't make the lines too close to the edge since this will look tight. Leaving a gap of about ½in (1cm), tape a second rectangle inside the first, cutting the tape with a pair of scissors to make square corners. The tape will stretch naturally so bend it slightly to make the line slightly irregular and not completely straight—although don't make too obvious curves.

2 Take a clean brush and dip it in the Old White paint. Wipe the brush gently on some paper to remove the wetness of the paint and dab it between the tape. Press firmly in some places and lightly in others so that the line is slightly uneven.

3 For the handpainted line choose a small area like the front of a drawer and use your little finger as a rest to keep your hand steady. Make a mixture approximately ⅔ paint and ⅓ water. It should be liquid enough to drip gently when you press a charged brush against the side of the paint pot. Dip the artists' brush lightly in the mixture, taking care not to pick up too much paint. Rest your little finger on the side of the drawer and slide it along the edge as you move the brush. The line won't be perfect but will be in character with old painted furniture.

Before

This little Victorian pine table probably was painted originally but had been stripped when I found it. Some time ago I began to give it back some character by painting it with Duck Egg Blue but had then abandoned it because I couldn't think of the right technique to make the most of it.

4 Apply a thin coat of clear wax to the table with a brush. Polish the surface all over with a cloth to give the table a smooth finish.

color-washed shelves

PAINTING OVER OLD GLOSS PAINT

These shelves are so pretty with their arched and curving sides. I really wanted to use them—but not only were they covered in white gloss paint, there was also another layer of dark brown paint underneath. I decided to keep the white gloss as a base and make a wash of soft blue over it.

Before
I often find really nice bits of furniture that have been painted in gloss paint, often white. I know I can't be bothered to remove the paint—it is a terrible job involving paint removers and scrapers.

YOU WILL NEED

- Coarse sandpaper
- Old White paint
- Provence paint
- Tablespoon to measure paint
- Paint tray
- Flat paintbrush for applying paint
- Cloth for wiping paint
- Tin of clear wax
- 1in (2.5cm) paintbrush for applying wax
- Cloth for polishing wax
- Château Grey paint
- Small artists' brush

TIP *Completely avoid stripping paint or varnish because it is far too time consuming, messy, smelly, and, above all, boring. I did need to sand these shelves with coarse sandpaper but only went as far as removing the loose paint and smoothing out chips.*

1 Rub down the piece with some coarse sandpaper to remove all the loose old paintwork. The sanding will allow the new paint to adhere well to the glossy surface by giving a better base on which to work.

2 The color I wanted to use is a soft pale shade of Provence blue. Using a tablespoon as a measure, mix together three parts of the Old White and one part of Provence paint to make the color I call Cricket.

3 Take a flat brush, as big as you can comfortably manage, and spread the paint mix evenly and thickly all over the piece. Focus on one area at a time and don't put a lot of paint in the corners. While the paint is still wet move on to the next step.

4 Using a cloth wipe some of the paint off the shelf, gently at first, until the right "wiped off" effect is found. Repeat the process all along the back of the shelves to make a continuous "wiped off" effect, taking care not to get too much of a build up in the corners. The idea is that the paint will look dragged on the shelves, while on the edges—where I wiped off more paint—there is a soft wash of color with the white coming through.

5 As the paint is thin it will dry quickly so you should be ready to wax the piece almost immediately. Apply a layer of clear wax and then polish the surface. Apply a second coat of wax to really protect the surface and take care to buff well.

6 Paint the sides of the shelves with Château Grey. While the paint is still wet take the end of a small brush and use it to scratch or draw into the wet paint to make marks—I used lines, crosses, and swirly spots in a random pattern. I did the same along the back of the shelves, too. Apply another coat of wax to really protect the piece and buff well.

cow parsley chest

USING PRINTING EFFECTS ON FURNITURE

Oak is one of the few bare woods I like to see, but I also love it when it is softened with Old White. Cow parsley is a pretty country flower with a distinctive shape and I felt it would transpose well into print. The appeal of handprinting is the uneven random quality that you can achieve, which I felt would work well with the oak.

Before
The shape of this old oak chest of drawers appeals to me because it has a sturdy functionality but also a lot of charm.

WHAT YOU WILL NEED

- Old White Paint
- Water
- Paint tray
- 2in (5cm) paintbrush for applying paint
- Cloths for removing excess paint and wax
- Card
- Graphite paint
- Matchstick
- Tin of clear wax
- 1in (2.5cm) paintbrush for applying wax

1 Mix ⅓ water and ⅔ Old White in a paint tray to make a paint with a runny consistency.

2 Paint the mixture onto the surface of the chest, one area at a time. Oak is a textured wood so make sure you reach all the grain with the brush.

3 Wipe off the paint with a cloth as soon as you can before it dries, to give you a wash effect.

TIP *Choosing the card for the printing is quite crucial. A very hard thin card won't print and a very soft one won't be easy to manipulate.*

I had a very vague plan before I started and had imagined one stem of cow parsley. I started to make this one where I thought it should go, and then carried on working until I had a few stems.

4 To print the cow parsley stems, tear off a reasonably strong piece of card from a cereal box or something similar. Tearing is better than cutting so the card edge is softer and more random. Load the brush with Graphite and dab the paint along the edge a couple of times so there is a good quantity of paint there.

5 Print the stems by pressing down lightly with the edge of the card, and then more firmly. Bend the card slightly to get the natural bend of the stem. You will need several lengths of card for different parts of the parsley. Change the card for a fresh piece when it becomes saturated—if it is too soft it will slip and print blurred lines.

6 Use the flat end of a matchstick to print the dotty flowers of the cow parsley. Dot them on randomly so that some are heavy and others not so pronounced. Remember less is more! Apply a layer of clear wax when you are finished to seal, protect, and give a good even finish.

7 Add a layer of clear wax with a brush to the drawers and handle and rub off any excess with a cloth to finish.

8 Once I'd finished the chest I found that it looked slightly insipid with the Old White top. When I initially began the project I considered three colors for the top so I referred back to these and opted for Graphite instead, and was much more satisfied with the result. This is a great example of how projects never have to be rigid and set, so can sometimes evolve as you go along.

crackle, gilding, and découpage

Here are several techniques and materials that will make your furniture stand out from the crowd. Use paint and varnish to give it an antique look, create a glint with metal leaf, work in a relaxed way with stencils, or decorate with paper cut-outs.

découpage chest

USING PRINTED MATERIAL TO DECORATE FURNITURE

The word découpage derives from the French word meaning "to cut out" and describes an old technique used to apply printed motifs to furniture. For this project I chose an old chest that I had painted a few years ago, which needed an update. I was still happy with the distressed look, so I felt a simple découpage treatment using a floral watercolor print would embellish it perfectly.

YOU WILL NEED

- Design from a print book or other source
- Scissors
- Water
- Sponge
- Water-based matt découpage medium
- 1 in (2.5cm) paintbrush for applying medium

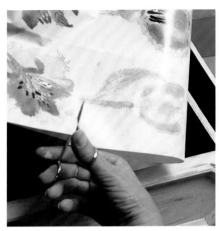

1 Cut out all your chosen prints using a pair of scissors, moving the paper rather than the scissors to keep the edge nice and smooth.

2 Take one of your cutouts and dampen both sides using a moist sponge to stop it from bubbling. Make sure you don't soak the paper by applying too much water.

3 Apply a coat of découpage medium to the front of the drawer where you want the design. Stick the paper down, starting at one end and pressing carefully so that no bubbles of air get trapped under the print.

4 Paint over the print with the medium to help to fix the design in place, then leave to dry. Add a second coat of medium and leave to dry. Repeat if necessary until you build up enough layers to give you a smooth surface.

TIP *Try using gift wrap for découpage since there are some really pretty and unusual prints in stores. Look out for watercolor patterns, these will give your finished piece a charming handpainted appearance.*

crackle-paint hooks

PAINTING MDF TO GIVE IT SOME CHARACTER

For me, the problem with MDF is that it lacks character and never develops with age in the way wood does. It is just too perfect so I like to find a way to give it some imperfections. This technique creates cracks in the paint and is a great way to lose the smoothness of the MDF finish. Chalk Paint® on its own applied thickly and then heated with a hair dryer cracks naturally. With a little practice you will be able to control the process, but don't try to aim for evenly sized cracks all over because this won't look natural. I chose a soft pink to go with the heart shape.

YOU WILL NEED

- Antoinette paint
- 2in (5cm) paintbrush for applying paint
- Hair dryer
- Tin of clear wax
- 1in (2.5cm) paintbrush for applying wax
- Tin of dark wax
- Small bristle brush for applying dark wax
- Cloths for removing excess wax

Before

This shelf, like many other new pieces of furniture, is made from MDF, or medium density fiberboard, because it is light, inexpensive, and easier to cut shapes from than natural wood.

1 Paint all over the shelf in Antoinette. This will act as a base for the second coat as MDF is very absorbent.

2 Once the first coat is dry, apply a second coat. This has to be done in a different way to the application of a normal coat of paint. Charge the brush well with paint then hold it nearly horizontal on top of the shelf and gently "lay" the paint on the surface. Work one small area at a time, applying the paint in a few different directions—but don't make it too busy. Add the paint more thickly on some areas than others.

3 Quickly use a hair dryer on the highest setting to blow hot air on the freshly wet paint. After a few seconds the paint should start to crack. If the paint goes into ripples instead then you are too near the surface or the layer of paint is too thick. It can be difficult to see what is going on so move your head around to see the surface in different lights. When you have finished one area move onto the next, until the whole piece is covered with smaller or larger cracks.

4 The paint is thicker than usual so make sure it is completely dry before applying the clear wax with a brush. Wipe off the excess with a cloth so there is a thin layer of wax.

5 Next apply the dark wax. This should be done with a small bristle brush, pushing the wax into the cracks by working the hairs in different directions.

6 Wipe off the excess dark wax with the cloth. You will find the dark wax is now in the cracks and will have changed the color of the paint too.

7 Take some clear wax and wipe it over the piece with a cloth to remove the dark wax from the surface, taking care not to remove any from the cracks. If any area is too cracked or busy then use the clear wax to remove some of the dark wax.

TIP *Do not confuse this crackle effect with "crackle varnish," a transparent varnish used over paint that cracks like the varnish on an old master painting. In the technique on these pages, the cracks are in the paint. There is a proprietary brand called Crackle Medium that can be used to achieve this look, but I prefer to use the hair dryer on the Chalk Paint®.*

crackle-varnish table

WORKING WITH TWO-PART CRACKLE VARNISH

I decided to paint this table in Old White in order to make it lighter and prettier. The technique used replicates the look of varnish that has cracked over time, like varnish on an old master painting. It is done with a set of two different water-based mediums, one laid over the other, that can be painted on any base color. I prefer to use it on Old White because it resembles aged ivory when finished. It is easier to apply the technique on small pieces of furniture, partly because it is difficult to control the materials over a large area.

YOU WILL NEED

- Old White paint
- 2in (5cm) paintbrushes for applying paint and Craquelure
- Bottle of Craquelure Step 1
- Bottle of Craquelure Step 2
- Hair dryer
- Tin of dark wax
- Cloths for applying wax
- Tin of clear wax

Before
This little round side table had an elegance that was unfortunately reduced by the country look of unappealing orange-varnished pine.

1 Start by painting the table all over with two layers of Old White. It is easier and more efficient if you turn the table upside down and paint the underside first.

2 Decide if you want to have larger or smaller cracks—if you apply the crackle varnish thinly you will end up with smaller cracks than if you apply it thickly. Apply a coat of Craquelure Step One to the surface of the table. Allow to dry naturally.

TIP Crackle varnish and crackle paint can be confusing as they have been given different names over the years. The previous project uses the idea of paint cracking, while this project is based on the application of two transparent varnishes, the second of which cracks. To achieve this look you need two bottles: the first is called Craquelure Step One and the second Craquelure Step Two. Both are transparent and allow you to see the wood base. It is a good idea to test them out first so you are sure about the right thickness of each of the varnishes. By applying them very thinly you will get small cracks.

4 Immediately after you have finished applying the second varnish, blow a hot hair dryer on the surface. After about a minute cracks will begin to appear—make sure the surface is in the right light so you can see them forming.

3 Apply the Craquelure Step Two with a brush. This is a viscous sticky varnish that can be a little difficult to spread, but be persistent and try to avoid lumpy, thick areas. As you are using a clear varnish it is easy to miss out areas so take care when applying.

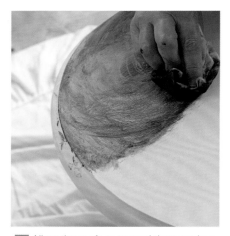

5 Allow the surface to cool then apply a layer of dark wax with a cloth, pushing the wax into the cracks. Work over the whole area but don't allow the wax to dry too hard otherwise it is difficult to remove. Wipe off any excess with a clean cloth.

6 Using a very small amount of clear wax, wipe off any dark wax lying on the surface, so that the dark wax is only left in the cracks.

découpage chest of drawers

CREATING A DÉCOUPAGE DESIGN AND ADDING COLOR

There are découpage motif books, but you could also find a good image in a magazine or online. The picture can then be adjusted, scanned, and printed using a computer. The paper design is then cut out and stuck down onto a surface and varnished several times. I have chosen a design of people running to go along each drawer.

Before

While in Venice some years ago I was inspired by the most charming 18th-century découpage cabinet with sepia prints on it, colored gently and haphazardly with watercolor. This chest of drawers was the perfect piece to emulate the effect I saw that day in the Doge's Palace.

YOU WILL NEED

- Design from a print book or other source
- Computer, scanner, and printer
- Scissors
- Water-based matt découpage medium
- 1in (2.5cm) paintbrush for applying medium
- Barcelona Orange paint
- Monet Blue paint
- Olive Green paint
- Water
- Small artists' brush
- Tin of clear wax
- 1in (2.5cm) paintbrush for applying wax

1 I have chosen a design of a hilarious medieval chase with skirts flying and arms waving that I saw in a book of découpage prints. After measuring the height of the drawers I scanned and enlarged the design to the required size. The initial printout was a little dark for my taste so I changed the color to a brownish black and printed it out again. I also reversed the design on the computer so that the people will be running the opposite way on the middle drawer. If you struggle with computers, take your chosen design to a local copy shop; they will be able to help you scan and print it out.

2 Cut out the figures with a sharp pair of scissors, getting as close to the edge of the design as possible. It's best if you cut everything out before you start glueing so you can plan roughly where you are going to position each figure. Next, paint the whole area of one drawer front with the découpage medium.

  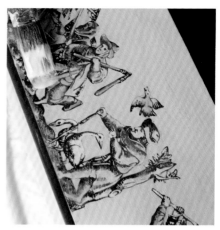

3 With the découpage medium still wet, place a cut-out figure at one end of the drawer. At the same time brush over the design with the medium, which will now act as a varnish. Try to avoid the paper bubbling up by brushing from one end to the other. If a bubble does come up try to press it down and out the side, but do this quickly before the varnish begins to dry. Repeat the process until the whole drawer front is filled with images. Varnish the drawer twice more, allowing each layer to dry thoroughly.

4 For the painting of the pictures choose one main color and two or three others to partner it. I selected watered down Barcelona Orange as my main color with some Monet Blue and Olive Green—one hot and two cool colors. I applied the colors to the "clothes," sometimes deliberately missing the area a little so it looks more like a painting. Use the paint like watercolor and make the color uneven in parts. If you make a mistake take the paint off with water.

5 When you've finished coloring, complete the drawers with two layers of varnish. Either wax the whole piece, including the drawer fronts, with a brush or continue with varnish—I prefer wax.

TIP *Try to avoid having a single small image in the middle of a drawer as it can look a little corny. If you have one good image perhaps try using it enlarged so it fills up the area.*

6 I painted my main color Barcelona Orange inside the drawers, which is in deliberate and strong contrast to the coolness of the outside decoration.

gilded wall stencils

USING REAL GOLD FOR A STUNNING EFFECT

Due to its position in the room this wall deserved special attention. I felt it would merit using a stencil design and real gold to attract the eye. The sheen and life in real gold is incredibly beautiful and without comparison to other forms of leaf. In keeping with my speedy approach to projects, I do not measure out the stencil to make it completely regular, even though here is a pattern that is repeated. I feel that if you want a unifrom print then use wallpaper instead—any slight irregularity makes the wall lively and interesting. Apply the paint by eye and fill in any gaps with part of the stencil.

WHAT YOU WILL NEED

- Stencil
- Old White paint
- Roller and paint tray
- Water-based gold size glue
- Small artists' brush for glue
- Gold transfer leaf
- Small artists' brush for applying leaf

Before

This wall was over a fireplace and was the focus of attention in the room, but was plainly decorated and boring to look at.

TIP *Real gold comes in many colors (see page 145) so you can choose a gold that works with your background. For my background I have used taupe, a gray brown that works well with the mid-tone and shade of gold I have picked.*

1 Place the stencil on the wall after working out roughly where you want the design to go. Using a roller and a small amount of paint lighter than the wall color—I chose Old White—mark out the stencil over the whole area you are working on.

2 Using a small brush apply the gold size to the areas you want to be gold. Once the size becomes clear it is ready for the leaf to be applied.

3 Use a dry brush to apply the leaf to the wall. Have a piece of tissue paper behind the leaf and press against it. This helps the leaf to stick to the size and not to the brush or your hands.

4 Wipe away any excess leaf with a soft but firm brush and then check your work for any areas you may have missed.

trumeau mirror

APPLYING BRASS LEAF TO CARVED DETAILING

This is a modern reproduction trumeau, a French style of mirror that traditionally has a painted or carved panel above or below the glass. Before starting, choose where you want your gilding to be. I have chosen to paint the frame in Duck Egg Blue in keeping with the style of mirror, but another color could work equally as well—perhaps white or gray, or a mixture of both.

Before
This type of mirror was often both gilded and painted, so is ideally suited for a paint transformation.

YOU WILL NEED

- Duck Egg Blue paint
- 2in (5cm) paintbrush for applying paint
- Water-based gold size glue
- Small artists' brush for applying glue
- Talcum powder (optional)
- Book of brass leaf
- 1in (2.5cm) paintbrush
- Small soft bristle artists' brush
- Tin of clear wax
- 1in (2.5cm) soft bristle brush for applying wax
- Cloth for removing excess wax
- Tin of dark wax
- 1in (2.5cm) paintbrush for applying dark wax

1 Paint all over the wood in Duck Egg Blue, taking care not to get paint on the mirror. Use a stabbing motion on the carved areas to ensure all the detailing is covered. You may have to apply a second coat to make certain the whole of the mirror is covered.

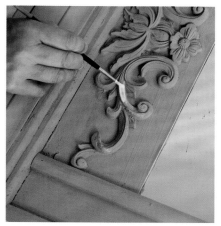

2 When the paint is dry take a small brush and paint the gold size glue onto all the areas where you want to apply the brass leaf. Be certain to cover everything completely and take care not to apply the gold size too thickly, or with drips and bumps. At first the gold size is white; leave it a few minutes and once it becomes clear it is ready to use.

3 Before using the leaf it is a good idea to dust your hands lightly with talcum powder to make them very dry, because the leaf will stick to your hands if they are slightly damp or sticky. Take a sheet of the brass leaf from the book—it doesn't matter which side faces up—and with one hand lay it on the area with the gold size. With the other hand press the leaf in place with a brush.

4 Use a small artists' brush to guide the leaf and lay it down as flat as you can, making it sure it has adhered well to the gold size.

5 Use the brush to push the leaf into the crevices, making certain it sticks really well to the surface so it won't come off at the next stage. Sweep away all the excess leaf you don't want with the brush.

6 Take a soft brush and wipe the gilded areas with a thin layer of clear wax, pushing the wax into the carving. Cover the rest of the mirror with the clear wax then wipe off any excess with a cloth. A clean soft brush will remove any excess in the carving, too.

7 Apply dark wax to the carved areas of the mirror using a brush.

8 Be gentle but try to push the wax into the corners of the carving so it looks as if it was age and dirt.

TIP *I have used brass leaf in this project as it is very inexpensive. Real gold leaf could be used but it is much more expensive. If you choose to use real gold you do not have to wax it because it does not tarnish like brass, but you will have to use the sheets in transfer form (see page 145).*

9 Use a cloth and/or a brush to wipe and spread the excess wax on the carving. This is best done using some clear wax because it acts as a kind of "eraser," taking away the dark wax and softly wearing away the "gold." The harder you rub the more leaf will be removed— it is up to you how much of the dark wax and gold you leave.

10 Using a dry brush stipple the area to take away any pockets of dark wax and make the finish more even.

real gold gilded tray

ADDING A DISTRESSED GOLD EFFECT TO DETAILING

This tray presented a perfect opportunity to use real gold leaf rather than brass leaf. Gold is, of course, more expensive than brass—but it's not out of the question to use it every once in a while, especially on a small project like this. Gold is unlike brass in that it doesn't tarnish if left exposed to air and will continue to look bright and lustrous; it's shine is mellower and deeper, too. I love the matt simple dry look of this tray and the gold is reminiscent of Swedish painted furniture.

Before

I bought this tray new because I liked the molded leaves and flowers around the edge, but I found it rather plain and decided to adorn it with some gilding.

YOU WILL NEED

- Water-based gold size glue
- Small artists' brush for glue
- Gold transfer leaf (not loose leaf)
- 1in (2.5cm) brush for applying leaf
- Pot of shellac or button polish (optional)
- Cotton cloth to apply shellac

1 Apply the gold size to the areas that you want to gild. When the size is first applied it will be white before becoming clear, at which point it is ready to be used. I have applied the size along edges and centers of the plant design rather than solidly over all the detailing.

2 Take a sheet of transfer leaf and place it gold side down on the gold size. Use one hand to hold the tissue and in the other use a dry brush to press the tissue and stick the leaf to the size. The carving is textured, which means the coverage of the leaf will not be completely even unless you are prepared to go over the same area many times.

3 With the dry brush, wipe away all the small pieces of leaf that are have not stuck to reveal the result of your work. At this point you can decide whether to leave it as it is if you want an old distressed look, or apply more size and leaf for a more solid gold effect.

4 This next step is not absolutely necessary, but I used a dab of shellac (sometimes called button polish) on the gold to help make it slightly darker and protect the work. This dries extremely quickly so put a little onto a cotton cloth, dab, and wipe once before moving to the next part.

TIP *One of the many attractions of real gold is that it comes in many colors, from very pale yellow to coppery red. Brass leaf comes in just one color. To work with gold you need to use it in the form of transfer leaf because loose leaf is too fragile to use without specialist equipment. Transfer leaf is a very thin sheet of gold very lightly "stuck" to a square of tissue. Gold does not tarnish so does not have to be sealed, but you may want to put a coat of shellac on it to protect it.*

1920s glass-fronted cabinet

MAKING ALUMINUM LEAF LOOK LIKE SILVER

Glass-fronted cabinets were very popular in the 1920s for displaying your best china. They have largely gone out of fashion now, but as pieces of furniture they look great with a little overhaul. Try using one in a bathroom for perfumes, creams, and soaps or, as I have done here, in the living room with a collection of glass cake stands and a jug also from the twenties. Black, glass, and silver is a color combination from the thirties that also has a contemporary feel, so I used a black ticking fabric for the inside, gilded the top edge with aluminum leaf, and covered the edgings with a black ribbon.

YOU WILL NEED

- Graphite paint
- 2in (5cm) paintbrush for applying paint
- Paper
- Sticky tape
- Water-based gold size glue
- 2 small soft bristle artists' brushes
- Book of aluminum leaf
- Small dry brush for applying leaf
- Tin of dark wax
- 1in (2.5cm) paintbrush for applying wax
- Cloth for removing excess wax

TIP *A little silver goes a long way so don't get too enthusiastic with it. I had contemplated doing the ball feet of this cabinet but in the end decided that less is more.*

1 Apply a coat of Graphite to the cupboard with a brush, but leave the edges that are next to the glass.

2 Cover the glass on the cabinet with paper, fixing it in place with tape, and paint the frame around the glass. Take care not to get too much Graphite on the paper and the glass. Change the paper when it gets too wet.

Before

This cabinet has lovely little ball-and-claw feet, a very stylish yet definitely shabby glass design on the door, and a delightful border running along the top. Traditionally these cabinets have fabric, or sometimes paper, on the back and floor, and true to form this piece had a very dusty, mottled fabric, which sadly had to be covered as it couldn't be rescued.

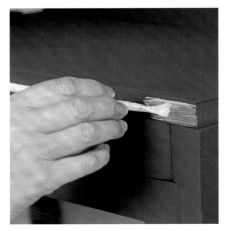

3 When the paint is dry, paint a thin layer of the gold size glue to the top edges of the cabinet. Take your time and avoid getting any glue on the top of the cabinet. Don't worry about the gold size drying out, it remains sticky for hours.

4 Leave the gold size to become transparent; this should take about five to ten minutes depending on the surface you are painting on.

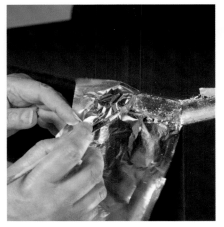

5 Apply the aluminum leaf by letting the leaf fall on to the gold sized surface. Use a small, dry brush to guide it and to flatten it onto the wood. Dab rather than wipe the brush to stop the leaf from breaking up. When the leaf is sufficiently stuck down, tear off the excess. It will not show where there is a join in the wood.

6 Using a brush, apply a layer of dark wax all over the top of the cabinet. This makes the previously dark gray paint turn a beautiful black. The aluminum turns from silver white to a lovely, slightly tarnished silver after the dark wax has been added.

7 While the wax is still wet wipe off the excess, working it into the paint. Take extra care along the edges so you don't damage the metal-leafed areas.

bureau with floral motif

STENCILING AN INTERIOR

Bureaux or desks like this have been out of favor for a while but recently have had something of a revival. This is because they are a good surface for using a laptop and when the lid is closed they have an understated, noble appearance. Everyone needs a place to keep paperwork and their computer and this is the elegant answer. Having the option to paint an interior is a great opportunity to apply a decorative pattern or use some extravagant color.

Before
The shape of this bureau, with its deep drawers and front, was just the solution I was looking for to help tidy my office.

WHAT YOU WILL NEED

- Château Grey paint
- 2in (5cm) paintbrushes for applying paint
- Cream paint
- Paris Grey paint
- Sponge roller and paint tray
- Stencil
- Tin of clear wax
- Cloth to apply the wax
- Medium-grade sandpaper
- Aubusson Blue paint (optional)

1 Paint the inside of the desk and the interior of the drawers with Château Grey. Often on the interior of a bureau there will be a surface of leather or something similar but don't worry, this can be painted over easily with the Chalk Paint®.

2 Paint the outside of the desk in a different color to the inside. You can either choose a very different color, bright red for instance, or something similar like the Cream I chose. Use a generous amount of paint brushed in different directions to give it texture. For authenticity, make some areas more textured than others.

3 Paint over the Cream with Paris Grey, this time quite smoothly and with a restrained amount of paint. Work in the same direction as the wood and leave to dry. This coat means that when you sand, the top layer of gray will come away easily to show the more uneven Cream marks underneath.

4 For the stenciling, pour two colors of paint, Cream and Paris Grey, into the tray then work the sponge roller so that one half is one color and one half the other. Don't get too much paint on the roller so that it becomes heavy with paint. If there is too much, roll the sponge out on a piece of spare paper.

TIP *Stenciling is a great way to make a pattern, but it is the random manner of application that is quite difficult to master if you are not used to it. It's best to stencil almost blindly, as if you are just trying to cover the area.*

Here I chose to use the same colors as the outside of the desk for the stencil and a deeper color for the base. For the stencil itself I picked two designs that are very similar in style, shape, and size. Flip the stencil over to vary the design.

5 Place the stencil down on the interior in your required position and start applying the roller gently keeping the pattern variegated. Apply the same stencil in lots of places all over the inside of the desk. Allow the stencil to dry—it should take about five minutes—and turn it over. The application of two colors on the roller at the same time and the turning of the stencil will help to make the pattern random.

6 Apply a layer of clear wax with a cloth to the whole piece and then lightly sand the surface. If you feel you need to adjust the coloring and pattern, you can add some extra color as I have with Aubusson Blue. I also covered over some areas with a bit of the base color, Château Grey, using the stencil. Finally, wax again and polish.

paint colors

Annie Sloan Chalk Paint® has been used in all the projects in this book. This is a unique paint in 24 decorative and historical colors made specifically for painting furniture and floors, and for giving walls a matt, velvety finish. Please visit my website to find your local stockist or for mail order details: www.anniesloan.co.uk.

Old White	Country Grey	Paris Grey	Duck Egg Blue
Antoinette	Old Ochre	Cream	Versailles
Louis Blue	Scandinavian Pink	Barcelona Orange	Sienna Yellow
Provence	Antibes Green	Monet Blue	Emperors' Silk

Primer Red

Graphite

Château Grey

Greek Blue

Aubusson Blue

Olive

Old Violet

Burgundian Red

suppliers

Annie Sloan Paints
www.anniesloan.com
paint@anniesloan.com

Annie Sloan Interiors
33 Cowley Road
Oxford OX4 1HP
Tel: 01865 247296
Open 9:30–5:30 Monday to
Friday, 9:30–1:00 Saturday

ENGLAND
Cornwall
Country Chic
4 Northgate St
Launceston
Cornwall PL15 8BD
Tel: 01566 773223
Chalk paint

Devon
Connybear Farm
St Marychurch Road
Coffinswell
Newton Abbot
Devon TQ12 4SE
Tel: 01803 875 615
www.connybearfarm.com
Chalk paint and courses

Gloucestershire
Bailey Paints
Griffin Mill Estate
London Road
New Stroud, Thrupp
Glos GL5 2AZ
Tel: 01453 882237
Chalk paint

Hampshire
Interior Affairs
6 The Grove
Westbourne
Emsworth
Hampshire PO10 8UJ
Tel: 01243 389972
Chalk paint and courses

Hertfordshire
Lavender Blue
18 London Road
St Albans
Hertfordshire AL1 1NG
Tel: 01727 839415
www.lavenderblueshop.com
Chalk paint and courses

Isle of Wight
Crocus
51 Union Street
Ryde PO33 2RF
Tel: 01983 611144
Chalk paint

Kent
Smoke on the Water
9 Market Street
Sandwich
Kent CT13 9DA
Tel: 01304 611600
www.smokeonthewater-
kent.co.uk
Chalk paint and courses

London
Sally Bourne Interiors
26 Muswell Hill Broadway
London N10 3RT
Tel: 020 8444 3031
www.sallybourneinteriors.
co.uk
Chalk paint and courses

Nottinghamshire
Design Works
16 Carter Gate
Newark
Nottinghamshire
NG24 1UB
Tel: 01476 570170
Chalk paint

Oxfordshire
Bliss Home Accessories
Station Mill Antiques &
Interiors Centre
Station Road
Chipping Norton
Oxfordshire OX7 5HX
Tel: 01608 644563
Chalk paint

Life at Nettlebed
1 High Street
Nettlebed
Nr Henley
Oxon RG9 5DA
Tel: 01491 642062
www.lifeatnettlebed.co.uk
Chalk paint and fabric

Suffolk
Painted Country
1 Castle Street
Eye
Suffolk IP23 7AN
Tel: 01379 871888
www.paintedcountry.co.uk
Open 10.00–4.00
Wednesday to Saturday
*Chalk paint, fabric, and
courses*

Wiltshire
Holt Barn Emporium
The Tannery
Holt
Near Bath BA14 6BB
Tel: 01225 782906
Open Thursday to
Saturday
Chalk paint